Masters
and
Disciples

Masters and Disciples

Hal Sarf, Ph.D.

CENTER FOR HUMANITIES
AND CONTEMPORARY CULTURE
&
REGENT PRESS
Berkeley

Library of Congress Cataloging-in-Publication Data

Sarf, Hal, 1941-2002
    Masters and disciples / Hal Sarf.
        p. cm.
    Includes bibliographical references.
    ISBN 1-58790-031-9
        1. Teacher-student relationships. Title.
LB1033 .S26 2002
371.102'3--dc21   2002068268

Manufactured in the U.S.A.

A Publication of the
**Center for Humanities and Contemporary Culture
& Regent Press**
6020-A Adeline Street
Oakland, CA 94608
510-547-7602
regentpress.net
regentpress@mindspring.com

Contents

NOTES

Acknowledgements

Although I am bedridden with paralysis on my right leg and arm, and with terminal metastatic cancer as my fate, I was determined to finish several books that were dormant on my computer, a machine I could no longer operate in order to complete my projects.

I wish to express my gratitude to Steve Keightley, my twenty-four hour Home Caretaker, for printing hard copies of my work for me to edit while I was sitting up in bed, for entering my corrections on the computer, and for bringing the copies to the publisher and retrieving the final proofs for me to correct. I am truly indebted to Steve for his invaluable help.

Much appreciation is due Professor Cherryl Smith for her precious time to proof read my manuscripts, for suggesting corrections, and for visiting when I was feeling low. I also thank her for bringing her excellent home made chicken soup, which lifted my dark doldrums.

Ted Feldman, my friend and former student, has lavished unconditional support for me in my darkest moments of despair, proving again and again to be a steadfast and loyal companion—a rare gift in this world of transient relationships. I am forever indebted to Ted.

Finally I wish to give my heartfelt thanks to Bryan Walker, also a former student, and to his lovely wife, Michelle, for their affection, good-cheer, and continuing kindness in the midst of my affliction. We have many conversations about life, death and meaning, and they are truly seekers of wisdom.

I would also like to thank friends and students too numerous to mention.

Hal Sarf, Ph.D.
May 2002

Introduction

The great Western thinkers achieved immortality through bequeathing concepts and values that evolved into enduring traditions of discourse about recurring civic, philosophical and ethical issues—traditions that may establish the limits and possibilities of discourse itself. Minds of the highest rank are often marked by a missionary zeal, believing they possess superior wisdom that when successfully disseminated, would transform thought and action to improve the human estate, ridding it of institutions, practices and values deemed harmful. Historical experience shows that most thinkers fail to refashion life to accord with their visions; only a select few offer theories and ideals that are akin to bright flames that illuminate the darkness of personal and collective life, standing as steadfast beacons in the changing currents of cultural and intellectual fashion that threaten to either dim or extinguish their lights. The usual fate of thinkers and their schemes of human and civic renewal, is obscurity born of the failure of memory to take root across the generations.

1

Fertile thinkers whose works survive the rise and fall of states and cultural fashion may owe profound, if sometimes anonymous debts, to disciples whose commentaries, codifications and revisions ensure that their ideas remain subjects of continuing conversation in the public realm. My book, then, examines the largely unexplored terrain of the master-disciple relationship to understand its complexities, benefits and dangers, thereby casting light on how traditions of thought are kept alive, enriched and perverted.

The master-disciple relationship occurs in all fields of knowledge—whether the arts, crafts, humanities, or social and physical sciences—where leading persons transmit ideas, methods and habits of cognition to learners. To realize fully the potentials of personhood, in contrast to other living beings, supposes the capacity to learn symbolic language and to be educated in patterns of thought and action by individuals with authority and knowledge, whether these are called masters, mentors, teachers, friends or parents. Persons molded through education are referred to by various names, whether learners, pupils, apprentices, students or disciples. Given the natural interdependence of dispensers of knowledge and those taught, issues arise about virtue and vice in the educational process when ideas, perceptions, methods, questions and moral judgments form the minds of the malleable.

My book addresses issues about inequality and

power, legitimate and tyrannical authority, freedom and coercion, truth-seeking and socialization, creativity and conformity, and asks why some teachers seek disciples and some learners want to be followers.

MASTERS AND DISCIPLES

CHAPTER ONE

Varieties of
Masters and Disciples

Teachers, Tutors, Mentors and Masters

What are the major varieties of educators and learners, and can ideal-typical forms of the master-disciple relationship be separated from those that mark the more common teacher-student bond? Do both have "normal" as well as "corrupt" patterns?

The teacher is clearly "one... whose function is to give instruction, especially in a school,"[1] that is, "to show how to" and to "present or offer to view."[2] Facts, concepts and methods are communicated by an authority who commands "what is to be observed or done" through "deliberate direction, prescription or enjoinment,"[3] being metaphorically akin to the "index finger... which points out; an indicator."[4] Good teachers, then, help students learn the principles of particular subjects, whether philosophy, algebra, history, auto mechanics, or weaving. Although teachers naturally "communicate something by way of instruction", they also "train" or "accustom to the use or practice of,"[5] using example and admonition to help the student apply abstract principles to actual problems and situations.

In drawing an ideal-typical picture, the "teacher" implies a *limited* relationship to students, being confined to communicating information and methods within his or her domains of expertise to learners who either are obligated or freely choose to learn specific subjects. However, teachers at the primary through high school levels often assume surrogate parental roles by helping to socialize children and adolescents into desired behaviors in addition to conveying basic reading, writing and mathematical skills. For students seeking advanced academic, technical or professional education, teachers are more impersonal and less forgiving, expecting adult learners to have good work habits, self-discipline and clarity about their vocational goals—in short, to accept responsibility for their failures and successes.

Teachers are expected to evaluate "objectively" the abilities and performance of their students, although in practice that ideal is not always attainable given the insoluable difficulties establishing exact criteria of fairness. Besides, there is a natural human propensity to allow positive and negative feelings to influence judgment, sometimes causing reason to be shaped by strong emotions. Teachers are not above giving good grades and personal support to "pet" students of questionable motivation and ability, and to downgrade others of true merit because they experience dislike toward them. Judgment is rarely even-handed in the imperfect world of human relationships.

In formal settings, teachers have institutional authority to initiate activities students must follow, whether writing papers, taking tests, or giving oral reports. Disobedience and inferior performance—whether real or imagined—brings penalties, including poor marks, probation or eviction from programs, whereas success brings good grades, honors and favorable letters of recommendation. Teachers, then, naturally exercise authority—authority combining legitimacy and power—and authority can be abused by tyrannical, disciplinary teachers who assume the role of "master" by trying to forge strong intellectual and emotional bonds among learners to their own persons, pet theories and methods, often at the cost of retarding the growth of independent judgment.

Another variety of educator is the *mentor [mentor]* or "advisor," derived from the Latin root *men [mon; monitor]*, "to remember, think, counsel."[6] Homer disguises Pallas Athena as Mentor, an Ithacan nobleman, who guides the young Telemachus through a time of trial; hence, the common noun for a person who serves as an "experienced and trusted counselor."[7] The mentor's special care and assistance is usually offered by an older, respected person whose wisdom, experience and good-will prepares him to be a judicious, wise confidant, "The friend sticks close, a Mentor worthy of his charge,"[8] and "the same Mentor, who really is a most sincere friend."[9] Sometimes the term is applied to a personified thing or supernatural power in the capacity of a guide, "The Bible should be our Mentor,"[10] or the *daemon* which Socrates spoke of as his mentor.[11]

The mentor's relationship to youths seeking advice involves greater intimacy and trust than often found in the more impersonal and common teacher-student relationship, and is not conditional on the learner having a bond of discipleship to him. Being a guide and friend, the mentor refuses to imprint doctrine on malleable youths, for he ideally respects the moral and intellectual autonomy of those seeking help at times of perplexity, recognizing they must ultimately walk their own paths in life, being free to accept or reject his counsel.

The *tutor* [L: *tutor*] in rare usage refers to a teacher or divinity who guards, defends and watches over those in his care, such as the "poore oppressed people whom God takes into his custodie to be their tutor."[12] A tutor, then, cares for his ward and earns respect befitting an educator with decidedly parental traits, "Tutour, a defender, he that hath charge to bring up a childe"[13]; and further, we must not fail to bestow "the honor that the children owe to their parents and tutors."[14] In Roman times tutors-at-law *[legitimi]* "administered the estate of a person legally incapable, failing the father"[15] and were also appointed for women who "had not husbands or fathers governe them."[16]

Also, the tutor is a variety of teacher "employed in the supervision and instruction of a youth in a private household,"[17] often retained by the wealthy to "travel abroad with one or more pupils,"[18] perhaps in the manner of "Aristobulus, a Periptatetick, who is said to have been Tutor to Ptolemy Philometer."[19] The private tutor, then, combines the roles of a special teacher with the traditional parental role of disciplining children, having a greater degree of personal attention than found in the more narrowly proscribed and common teacher-student relationship.

The term tutor in a formal institutional setting was first employed at Oxford, Cambridge and Dublin to refer to "a graduate (most often a fellow of the College), to whom the special supervision of an undergraduate (called his pupil) is assigned."[20] Among the early duties of the tutor *[informator]* at Oxford in the sixteenth century was the collection of payments (creancer) from assigned pupils *[foundationer]* due their halls or colleges in accordance with Wykeham's Statutes. Eventually, the tutor's responsibilities expanded to include supervising the overall progress of his pupils' studies and living conditions, "That all persons of whatever quality soever, untill they be admitted to the Degree of Bachelor of Arts... does live under the care, tuition and instruction of approved tutors."[21] The undergraduate or "scholar" was also called the "tutor's pupil," and in the *Latin Statutes of Clare Hall* (1551) at Cambridge, the tutor is "a fellow of the College who... is responsible for his pupil's expenses, to explain to him what he has to do to learn, and... is to be treated with filial obedience and respect."[22]

If the tutor's grant of institutional authority carries elements of parental power, then he may act the part of a commanding "master" who demands obedience under threat of punishment, "Every master...is also a tutor and every boy must have his tutor... every exercise the pupil does is first submitted to the tutor for inspection and correction and then carried into school."[23] Tutoring, then, imparts culture, i.e., mental formation, through the teaching of precepts and methods, as in "an old Capuchin tutoring a novice"[24] because "his mind is not yet tutored to the philosophy of the subject."[25] Discipline—whether correction, admonition or sanction—is the tutor's tool to foster good intellectual and personal habits conducive to learning.

At contemporary Oxford and Cambridge a good deal of undergraduate education is the preserve of officially appointed tutors, and in American Universities and Colleges the tutor is often a graduate teaching assistant subordinate to a professor and appointed for a limited term of service. Also, a tutor can be a "private teacher" hired directly by students—sometimes made available through University auspices—

needing help in mastering difficult subjects, writing papers and preparing for examinations. Hence, tutors in philosophy, physics, political science, chemistry or law. In less common usage the tutor is analogous to a sophistical "coach" who teaches "one what to do or say" for the self-serving purpose of tampering with the truth when presenting evidence or being a witness.[26]

A person in a "tutored" condition ideally is intellectually and emotionally disciplined, "Seneca... had tutored himself to endure personal injuries without indulging in anger"[27]; and further, a tutored individual is able to guide others with authority and insight: "Our blessed second Adam hath our stock in guiding and he tutors it better,"[28] and "his tutor'd pen... would still repair the ruin of my name."[29] Lacking a tutored spirit, the individual may fall into sloth, is without clear direction in life, and is torn by the free-play of turbulent desires, "He was indulgent, almost frolicsome, in contradistinction to Mr. Whitfield's tutorly sharpness."[30]

The term *master* is rich in meaning, traditionally referring to a person of superior power, knowledge, skills, social rank, and, in the guise of the teacher, is positioned to attract disciples and to found a school or cult in which he is the center of attraction.

The Latin word *magnus* [Gk: *megas (megas)*; Sans: *mah*] means "great," and was used in reference to famous kings or nobles known for their special insight and great deeds, or to persons with exemplary artistic or intellectual abilities that mark them as "leading persons."[31] *Magis*, a contraction of *magnis* (from *magnus*) conveys the senses of "more," "greater quantity," and "most powerful."[32] *Magister*, the Latin root of the German "Meister" and English "Master", signifies "A man having direction or control over the action of another or others; a director, leader, chief, commander; a ruler, governor."[33] A master has authority to initiate actions that others complete, and in older usage, is a person who "employs another in his service."[34] The weaker party—whether the "servant," "man," "apprentice" or "student"—is a subordinate whose survival and well-being depend on the master's good-will: "Who's master, who's man,"[35] and "A master may by law, correct his apprentice..."[36] at least in traditional age. Indeed, the master's power may pass beyond material control and extend to the moral and spiritual formation of his dependents according to his own brand of *paideia*: "The old Proverbe is true... 'such a master, such a servant,'"[37] even though the result can be undesirable, "the general corruption of manners in servants is owing to the conduct of masters."[38]

"Master" is also an obsolete title for an "owner" or "possessor" of property with the "power to control, use or dispose of something at will."[39] Having the legal right to manage his holdings as he sees fit, whether inanimate or "living property"—horses, dogs or slaves—the master is that person to "whom an animal is accustomed to obey."[40] The owner regulates the activities of inferiors, and punishes for disobedience, "An unruly horse checked by a master's hand."[41] The male head of a household—the "Master of a family that wholly depended upon his life"[42]—expected that his wife and offspring defer to his authority or risk discipline since the "master of the house begins first."[43]

In older usage "master" also denotes the "head or presiding officer of... societies or institutions: e.g., of certain colleges (in Oxford, Cambridge and elsewhere), guilds, corporations, livery companies...,"[44] also being a "specific title of office" to "refer to dignitaries of monastic and other religious organizations...,"[45] whether the "master of Balliol College,"[46] "the master of the Temple-Church in London,"[47] "the master of the court," "the master of the Chancery," "master of the King's Bench," and "master of the Exchequer."[48] The title master, then, is applied to persons of high social rank or birth, prestigious office, great learning or rare skills, and implies having authority to command, at least in societies that affirm natural divisions exist between the intelligent and ignorant, the noble and base, and those due veneration from persons destined to bestow it.

"Master" traditionally was "freely affixed to all kinds of designations of persons, with the sense of 'chief', 'leading', 'commanding,'"[49] as in master-carpenters, master-tradesmen, master-barbers, master-artists, master-criminals, or master-teachers. Every variety of master possesses excellent traits, skills and capacities: "And last the master-bowman, he would cleave the mark,"[50] and "He's the master-criminal who can defy the law."[51] Also, "master" is rhetorically used to designate that aspect of material and immaterial things which qualify them as "main," "principal" and "controlling," as in "This is Satan's master-argument,"[52] and that is how that "rare dissembler... played his master-game...."[53]

The term "master" is used specifically in the arts, crafts and trades to designate a highly skilled practitioner who may have "others in his employ" as "distinguished from an apprentice or journeyman."[54] As the leading light, the master is "qualified by training and experience to teach apprentices and to carry out trade on his own account" whereas his subordinates are subject to his authority and directives.[55] Guilds of masters in medieval Europe controlled the professional trades and crafts, and apprentices might—after painstaking learning under their watchful eyes—become journeymen, and eventually gain mastership by producing *Meisterwerke* to prove their skills and right to independent practice.

In painting, sculpture and music we sometimes speak of "old masters" who lived before the modern era in the thirteenth through seventeenth centuries that aspiring art students ought to study to avoid thoughtless imitation of the transient styles and themes of the contemporary scene—assuming that traditional masters alone serve as the highest examples of excellent aesthetic form. After all, "Great Masters in Painting never care for drawing People in the Fashion" of the times, and a sensitive painter and intelligent painter "ought to attentively to consider... all the different styles of the great masters."[57]

The *magister* (master) in the medieval academic sense was a person "who has received a specific degree, originally conveying authority to teach in the university,"[58] and further, the student's writing of an approved thesis—the rough equivalent of the *Meisterwerk*—proved he was no longer a dependent learner but a master himself worthy of being a colleague. In English education prior to the nineteenth century, the term "master" was applied to persons studying in the Faculty of Arts to obtain an *artium magister*—the master of arts—with the "corresponding title in the other faculties being doctor."[59] In antiquated English school practice the "master" is "a teacher; one qualified to teach," and the term conveyed respect for "a man of approved learning, a scholar of authority"[60] to whose "care a child or children are committed for purposes of instruction."[61] The professional teacher was titled "master" because of the special trust of aiding the parents raise their young and to form their moral character, work habits and intellectual capacities: "I was bred myself, Sir, in a very great school, of which the Master was a Welshman,"[62] and received the "advice of one of our great master's in the science of life and morals."[63]

Possessing a higher degree and the title "master" hardly ensures having virtue and wisdom, for a corrupt master might do great harm by malforming the youths in his care. Further, a student in relationship to a master may be less a *pupillus*, or learner, and more a *servus* manifesting the qualities of a tail-wagging underling to an especially strong-willed master, that is, to a *Herr or dominus*.

The master can also be a *hierophant* [L: *Hierophanta*; Gr: *hierophantes (hierophantes)*], a religious or cult leader who "brings to light, makes known or reveals *[phanein]* what is esoteric and sacred *[hiero]*," and who also guards these from persons to whom revelation is not suitable.[64] In ancient Greece the hierophant was the "official expounder of sacred mysteries or religious ceremonies; an initiating or presiding priest,"[65] such as the "hierophant in the Eleusinian mysteries."[66] Claiming superior knowledge of the gods' will, and especially blessed by them, hierophants conduct secret rites for initiates who cannot grasp their true meaning without guidance from "the crafts of their heathenish Priests and Hierophants."[67] The hierophant, then, is the medium for divine insight, indeed, the voice of the god made audible to the chosen, "I listen to the Sibyl's chant, the voice of priest and hierophant."[68]

As protector and "interpreter of any esoteric principle," the hierophantic master broadly includes any person who claims possession of rare knowledge and the ability to convey it to the untutored, "poets are the hierophants of an unapprehended inspiration," and "the hierophant and interpreter of the Godlike in the soul."[70] A hierophant, then, manifests unusual traits of character and vision—a sacred allure—that sets him apart, "He, grand, calm, handsome, hierophantic, solemnly exhorted all men to constancy and courage."[71]

What essential quality is shared by every master, whether a superior teacher, painter, businessman, philosopher, hierophant or army general? The Latin verbal form, *magistrare* (to master) offers some clues. A person achieves excellence by "mastering" what stands in opposition, "To get the better of, in any contest or struggle; to overcome or defeat. With material or immaterial subject or object."[72] What is subdued might be another person's rebellious will, material that defies being shaped, or a demonic spiritual force that threatens well-being. If mastering means "to reduce to subjection, compel to obey, to break, tame (an animal),"[73] then what resists is utterly defeated, losing its power of self-determination: "They...swore to be obedient...so long as he maistered and kept them under,"[74] and "Every wise man masters his passions"[75] by forcing these to bend to the dictates of reason. If the adversarial force proves to be the more powerful, then the attempt to master will fail, "Deep grief masters me"[76] and neither "Kings nor authority can master fate"[77]—the latter offering a lesson that the vain ought to take to heart.

Strong-minded masters may view students as resistant spirits to be broken before they are sufficiently malleable to be molded according to their own educational precepts. A master who is "accustomed to...having one's own way," often is "imperious, self-willed, overbearing... high-handed, despotic, arbitrary."[78] Subtly alternating the use of friendly overtures and punishing actions toward students may keep them off balance and help the master "take possession of," "to own...," or "have at one's disposal" those under his charge.[79] An imperious master is akin to a *kurios*, "a lord who exercises power," or to a *despotes*, "one who has absolute ownership, an uncontrollable power." Insofar as a master feels compelled to dominate students, he stands in sharp opposition to the mentor who, while possessing and communicating knowledge, respects their personal dignity and moral autonomy.

"Mastering" also denotes successful learning, "To make oneself master of (an art, science etc.): to acquire complete knowledge or understanding of (a fact or proposition), or using (an instrument etc)."[80]

Learning is a great struggle if what is to be known or manipulated is elusive and complicated, or beyond the reach of a student with limited intellect and will power. "Mastering," then, brings into control through understanding or action that which initially stood apart as "other": "A boy has... mastered his Syntax,"[81] and "Grammar, rhetoric, Latin prose and poetry... she mastered ere she was grown up."[82]

Of course what is to be mastered might lay outside the preserve of traditional school subjects, as in the "instrument you have to master stands before you—the soul of man."[83]

Students, Disciples, Epigones and Sycophants

What are the significant conceptual differences between types of learners?

The Latin verb studere means "to be eager about," "to be diligent," "to study" and "application to learning"[84]; and further, "to strike at" or "aim at something," namely, gaining expertise in a subject matter.[85] Ideally, the student is one "engaged in or addicted to study"[86] and stands in a subordinate relationship to a teacher who sets academic standards and judges performance to be "excellent," "good," "brilliant," "average," "poor," or downright "awful." For example, it is expected that "the courteous and favorable student of art, ought to know the several sorts and kinds of Antinomy,"[87] and that the music student should "sing, or play...this scale of Do, until he is thoroughly familiar with the sound of it."[88] Learning is not an easy task and even the most diligent student may suffer fatigue, "Lest this hard student should one time or other crack his Brain with studying."[89] Although the term "student" denotes any type of learner in relation to a teacher, whether that teacher be a parent, mentor, friend, spouse or life-experience, a formal student is one "who is undergoing a course of study... instruction at a University or other place of higher education or technical training."[90]

In my preferred usage, the term "student" is correlative with "teacher" whereas "disciple" belongs with "master," although it is obvious that the ordinary teacher-student interaction provides the essential experiences from which may arise—but with no inevitability—the master-disciple relationship. I define a master as a special category of teacher who creates fashions, theories and methods that may—whether by design or not—attract disciples who imitate, propagate and defend these as their own; and further, is the pivotal figure around whom identifiable schools spring that may endure across generations. A teacher is one who authoritatively instructs students in one or more

subjects but with no intention of recruiting followers, forming schools, or cultivating strong intellectual
and emotional bonds among them. In short, every
master-educator is at bottom a teacher because knowledge is imparted to others, but not every teacher is a
master given the absence of impulse or capacity to
turn students into disciples.

What exactly is it to be a disciple?

The root of discipulus (disciple) in Latin is discere,
"to discern or learn,"[91] signifying that the disciple is
one who "follows or attends upon another for the purpose of learning,"[92] whereas the magister (master) is
that person "whose disciple one is; (in religion, philosophy, art, science or scholarship) from whom one
has chiefly learned, or whose doctrines one accepts."[93]
If masters attract followers and sometimes form cults
identified with their ideas, styles, methods and persons, it follows that the disciple is "one who belongs
to the school of any leader of thought"[94]: the "ceiling
is painted in fresco by Francesco Romanelli, a disciple of Peter of Cortona,"[95] and that "advanced The-
ist, of the school of the late Professor Green, of whom
he was a pupil and is a disciple."[96] For their part,
disciples are often proud to acknowledge their allegiance to particular masters, "I am one of your disciples and endeavor to live up to your rules."[97]

The Greek verb manthanein "to learn," (from root
math) implies "thought accompanied by endeavor,"[98]

of "adapting oneself, preparing for, growing accustomed" and "to acquire, adopt."[99] The pre-Socratics, Plato and the practitioners of mystery religions used the term in the double sense of attaining theoretical knowledge and purging the psyche of ignorance, error and evil, thereby turning the learner toward truth. Mathetes, the word for "disciple" and "learner", is a person who attaches himself to a didaskolos [didaskalos] to gain knowledge, whether an apprentice learning a trade, a student pursuing the medical arts, or a member of a philosophical sect seeking wisdom. Besides learning the theories and methods of a master on whom he is intellectually and emotionally dependent, the mathetes can be his personal companion and imitator; and even when the master dies the disciple may continue to experience his own spiritual identity as entwined with the haunting image of his didaskalos.

The disciple "follows" a master. But what is it to follow another? The Greek word akolouthein "to follow," comes from keleuthos, "a path," and means to "go somewhere with someone, accompany; to go behind." Also, the term metaphorically signifies "grasping what is said," "following the drift," "agreeing with someone's opinion," "adapting,"[101] and further, denotes a wise person who harmonizes with, and attends, the revelations of divinity, the eternal ethical standards of the cosmos, or the rational laws governing life. Just as the master finds his own spiritual direction by having special disclosures from something or someone both outside and greater than himself, so the disciple finds his center in life by walking behind the master on the path he marks outs.

Disciples may also parrot masters. Mimeisthai means "to imitate," "to mimic," to "emulate with joy," and "to follow" in the sense of simulating.[102] As a mimetes, the disciple imitates his master's words, deeds and even personal mannerisms to achieve superior understanding and direction. Judged to be the repository of goodness, wisdom and heroic virtue, the master is a model worthy of imitation; and although mimesis is perhaps an essential stage in learning, it can result—if not passed beyond—in a pathetic and personally destructive aping of another, signaling a spirit that lacks the will or capacity to follow itself.

Successful masters clearly "discipled" their students—to use the archaic verbal form which means "to teach, train, educate," "to make a disciple of," and to "convert to the doctrine of another."[103] For example, Jesus "discipled" the original Twelve to his teaching and authorized them to preach the "glad tidings" to gentiles and Jews: "Discipling disciples... such as have a calling to call others unto Christ...,"[104] and "Go out with zeal, disciple all mankind."[105] Disciples who actively "disciple" are fervent missionaries whose highest duty is to persuade others to accept the intellectual, ethical and spiritual truths of their masters.

Disciplinia [discipline] denotes the "instruction imparted to disciples"[106] under threat of correction and punishment meted out directly by the master or by those sanctioned to act on his behalf, "Fraile youth is oft to follie led... that better in vertues discipled,"[107] and "Alban... who strongly discipled in Christian patience, learnt his tortures to appease."[108] Wise masters recognize that their teaching is difficult to impart fruitfully unless their adherents achieve suitable mental and emotional habits; and further, the threat of discipline teaches followers to manifest beliefs and practices that identify them as belonging to particular philosophical schools, religious sects or political groups. Disciplinia, then, means "instruction having for its aim to form the pupil to proper behavior; the training of... subordinates to orderly action... mental and moral training."[109]

The "power of censure, admonition, excommunication..."[110] is exerted when conformity is not forthcoming, as discipline is the "order maintained and observed among pupils, or other persons under control or command."[111] Discipline, then, serves to protect the master and his loyal followers against errant belief and punishment, or the threat of it, and may bring rebellious individuals "to repentance and reformation of life."[112] After all, "Every sorrow and pain is an element of discipline"[113] and, especially for religiously-inclined spirits, "The present life was intended to be a state of discipline for a future one."

Wayward disciples always pose thorny problems for tightly-knit groups controlled by strong willed masters, and especially troublesome is the apostate. Apostasia in Latin means "desertion of one's faith... revolt, defection... literally a 'standing off...,'"[115] and the "abandonment of principles or party generally."[116] As a rebel and renegade, the apostate actively renounces the ideational and practical precepts of the master, and he is judged an evil person worthy of revulsion and expulsion because he "pursued his private interests by sacrificing those of his order...."[117] As a former "insider," the apostate is potentially quite dangerous because he possesses knowledge to expose the master's character flaws, the group's dirty laundry, and to give effective criticism of doctrine. Mastership clearly involves perils, for sometimes disciples become disillusioned and disobedient, leaving the fold filled with anger at feeling deceived and harboring negative thoughts against a leader once believed to possess the gospel truth.

The term acolyte [med. L: Acoluthus, Acoluth) denotes a disciple "in the Church who attended the priests, deacons, and performed subordinate duties, as lighting and bearing candles."[118] The acolyte, then, provides service: "Acolites, which waited with the Taper ready lighted,"[119] and at "every porch a priest came out with Acolyte and choir."[120] As a dependent "novice" commanded by a superior in the Church hierarchy, the term "acolyte" is metaphorically used to "designate the smaller of two stars placed in close proximity."[121] In a broad sense, any disciple who attends a master—running errands, caring for his household, giving money, arranging meetings or propagandizing on his behalf— is an acolyte akin to a planet orbiting around a large, central sun on which it depends for warmth and stability.

The term sycophant [L: sycophanta; gk: sukophantes] in ancient Athens originally designated a "class of men who were universally odious; the informers, or sycophants... who had perverted the laws."[122] Posing threats to the moral fabric of the civic order—"Who can scape the poisoned lips of slanderous sycophants?"[123]—sycophants are persons of low character who engage in sly dealings and false accusations for a price: "Men (says Xenophon) whom everyone knew to live by making calumnious accusations called Sycophancy."[124]

If the sycophant is something of a parasite, a "servile, clinging... abject flatterer,"[125] then he cultivates favor from the powerful by telling them what they wish to hear: "Such is his [the Pope's] power, attributed to him by his sycophants, that there can be no saints but of his own making,"[126] and "the young monarch was accompanied by a swarm of courtly sycophants."[127]

A powerful if insecure master may actively attract fawning, sycophantic disciples to reinforce his weak ego, to legitimate questionable doctrine, and to parrot his personal prejudices, sometimes relying on trusted and ardent followers to recruit new members to his cause, "crowds of spies, parasites and sychophants will surround the throne under the patronage of such Ministers."[128] Shrewd masters may use sycophants to further their own interests as the situation demands, whether to deflect blame for wrong-headed policies or to disseminate misleading information to rivals to disguise their true intentions as part of a cunning political strategy, "the real sentiments of this great prince... were very different from those of his sycophants."[129]

Still, the sycophant's loyalty to a master is inherently unstable; he may betray him as the winds of fortune change, whether to attain greater financial reward and prestigeful office, or as a prudent response to a shifting political situation, "upon sycophantic knees they bowed before the conquerer."[130] The sycophant is a spiritual relative of some sophists berated by Plato for using attractive rhetoric to persuade the citizens to dubious public policies, and for teaching their students what they wished to hear at the expense of truth to gain money and power: hence, "the bended knee of sycophant servility,"[131] and "the protector, now affecting kingship, is petitioned to take the title on him by all his new made sycophant Lords."[132] Cleverness and opportunism mark the sycophant, "it was... by flattery or sycophancy...that Haman had insinuated himself into the King's favor,"[133] and in democratic contexts "the people, like the Despot, is pursued with adulation and sycophancy."[134]

Moral baseness is not limited to the sphere of politics but occurs in every field of human endeavor, whether the office worker who climbs the ranks by sleeping with a detested superior, the fawning graduate student who against his better judgment prudently embraces the dubious pet theories of his dissertation director to secure a signature for the Ph.D., and aid in finding an academic post; or an aspiring writer who shamelessly mimics the style of a famous contemporary, hoping to ride the wave of popular fashion to attract a publisher.

Disciples sometimes congregate into a cult [L: cultus]—a group of persons engaged in common "worship, devotion and homage"—the term "cult" formed from colere which means "to inhabit, cultivate, protect, attend to, and honor with worship."[135] Kwel, the hypothetical etymological root of cult, signifies to "be or move habitually (in or with)"; and colonus denotes "tiller, cultivator, planter, settler."[136] Kuklos denotes to "move around, to be occupied with" and polos refers to an "axis" or "pole."[137] A cult, then, is a gathering of persons sharing a special place where "rever-

ential homage" is "rendered to a divine being, or beings," such as "that portion of the Roman Church
which is devoted to the cultus of the Blessed Virgin."[138]
The cult-master, whether person or god, is the sacral
center or the metaphorical wheel-hub to which the
disciples—the separate spokes—are connected, signifying that they gain their center and strength by join-
ing to their object of veneration.

Although cults vary in types of masters, and in
their beliefs and practices, most have antipathy to outside inspection given their strict criteria for membership, being the preserve of initiates "devoted in their
attentions to the objects of their cult."[139] And if cults
pay "homage to a particular person or thing,"[140] then
we should "Let not every circumstantial difference or
variety of cult be named a new religion"[141] given that
cults are wholly unlike the major religions which pride
themselves on being open and inclusive. A cult, then,
is a "body of professed adherents" who are "Convin'd
of the reality of a better Self"[142] by virtue of being
instructed by, and paying homage to, a master—
whether god or person.

Cult aspirants undergo a process of cultivation [L:
cultivat, cultivare], much as the earth is tilled [cultiva
terra] by farmers with the aim of "improving and rendering fertile."[143] Initiates of cults are akin to seeds or
young animals that require proper tending by the master and his chosen subordinates; they attempt to im-

plant "Manners with good precepts and Counsels"[144] and may seek to weed out the "wild licentious with Wisdom, Discipline and Liberal arts."[145] Once the desired habits of thought and action are learned, cult members are transformed into "true believers" who actively promote "the advancement or development of (an art, science, sentiment, habit or pursuit)" with the "object of... improving oneself in it."[146] Clearly, cults are powerful mediums of forming self-identities, values and practices.

Cultivare also means seeking the "friendship or good opinion of another,"[147] and "to bestow attention upon...with a view to intimacy or favour...."[148] If the cult-leader is perceived by his disciples as powerful, wise and surrounded by a sacred allure, then being close to him is quite desirable to star-struck devotees. And if "The great honour him, cultivate him, respect him, court him,"[149] it is reasonable to expect lesser lights to do the same. Culture [L: cultura], the past pluperfect stem of colere, has the archaic meaning of "worship" and "reverential homage," as in "when thy departe fro thy culture and honour their god."[150] Paying homage is culture for the disciple, the act that affirms his belonging to a superior order of life and activity.

The term "culture" is also a synonym for cultivare (cultivation), "such a plot of his Eden... gratefully crowns his Culture... with chaplets of flowers,"[151] and "England is far too North for the culture of the vine."[152] With respect to persons, culture denotes "the development of the mind, faculties and manners; improvement or refinement by education and training."[153] If masters "culture" disciples for "the... profit of theyr myndes,"[154] and if Hobbes is correct that "the education of children is... a culture of their minds,"[155] then potential cult members are akin to the very young whose reason and emotions require proper formation to reach maturity. As the condition of being cultured varies according to the standards employed, it follows that disciples socialized into a particular cult often experience a rival one as "a language and culture... wholly alien to them,"[156] indeed, as error-laden and threatening given the fact that "our minds are not all formed or cultured alike."[157]

Disciples may also belong to sects [L: secta; used as cognate object in sectum sequi] defined as "a body of persons who unite in holding certain views differing from those of others...of the same religion..." but "deviating from the general tradition."[158] A sect, then, is a minority religious body "having a distinctive name and its own places of worship,"[159] having separated from the orthodox beliefs and rituals of its parent organization, e.g., as "applied by Anglicans to the various bodies of Dissenters, and by Roman Catholics to all forms of Protestants."[160] Regardless of their individual traits, sects are seen by mainstream organizations as schismatic, splinter groups. As with cults, devotees of sects adhere to a special "system of belief or observance"[161] and "follow a particular course of conduct... or a person's guidance or example."[162] Secta in medieval Latin denoted "the distinctive costume of a class or order of men"[163] that set them apart from ordinary humanity: "my sect thou seest, now learn too late how few... may know, when thousands err."[164] Wearing special dress or having other unique signs are exterior expressions of an inward condition of mental conformity to a revered leader, doctrine and way of life.

Sects are often objects of vicious gossip, persecution and sometimes outright destruction by the orthodox that label their offspring "apostate" for renouncing customary belief and practice, as demonstrated in the religious strife of the Reformation: "the damnable opinions of the secte of the anabaptistes,"[165] and "they that love sectes are indede worthy of punyshement."[166] To the orthodox faithful, the offshoot group threatens unity, having "made a little sect of itself" by "entertaining peculiar tenets of its own,"[167] clearly "the common practice (at least among the Sects) of declaring against reason as an enemy to Religion."[168] As with cults, sect members are deeply attached to their views, leaders and institutions, often showing a fanatical self-righteous spirit and seeing themselves persecuted by hostile unbelievers or followers of false religions. For their part, the mainstream groups judge the splinter ones to be deserving of persecution, "The Pharisee was a sectarian, one that deviated... in his worshipping from the way of God,"[169] and "the Queen of England hated Anabaptists, Calvinists and other sectarians," thinking these posed threats to the Kingdom's stability.[170]

Sects sometimes are fostered by charismatic philosophers around whom disciples congregate, defend and parrot, believing they are party to esoteric wisdom, "three of the most learned that ever professed the Platonicke sect,"[171] and "Our poet was a Stoick philosopher... and all his moral sentences are drawn from the Dogmas of that Sect."[172] Although it is debatable whether "the "sect of the Stoics" was the "purest and most exalted philosophical sect of antiquity,"[173] or whether "that sect of men of letters in France who call themselves the Economists"[174] actually attained knowledge of the obscure laws governing production and exchange, it is certain that "Sect leaders their own visions may impose"[175] and that "he who receives revelations becomes a sect-founder."[176] To unsympathetic outsiders, the sect-master is a dangerous charlatan worthy of suppression for having discipled the unwary into false beliefs, "ther came immediately false apostles and sectemakers, drue every man discipled after hym,"[177] and "a general feeling of alarm and suspicion broke out against the sage Pythagoras and his sectarians."[178]

The term sectarian denotes a particularly fanatical disciple as used in the English Commonwealth period by Presbyterians to deride Independents who threatened stable political and religious order: "that sectarian armie now infecting this Kingdome"[179] whose Non-Conformist members were not above "Drawling out the words of Scripture with deep sectarian drone."[180] Sectary [Med. L: sectarius; also L: sectator; sectatour] —an obsolete synonym for sectarian—refers to a "bigoted adherent"[181] of a sect: "Sectary! those who dissent from the domineering party have always been thus stigmatized."[182] If "Shakespeare is no sectary" because "he deals with equity and mercy,"[183] then the sectary-spirit lacks tolerance, magnanimity and compassion: "every zealous sectary adheres to his own exclusive doctrine,"[184] and "John...exhibited sometimes the narrow spirit of the sectary."[185] It is clear to detractors that "many sectaries experience much inhuman treatment,"[186] given that "the arts that civilize society are not calculated for men who mean to rise on the ruins of established order."[187] Clearly, the sectary is alienated from mainstream institutions, values and practices, and seeks basic changes in the social and religious fabric of life to usher in a transfigured world: "Now I am discontented, Ile turne Sectarie, that is fashion,"[188] and "those sectaries who are present at work upon the destruction of the orthodox churches."[189]

A sectary is also a "votary of a particular study,

pursuit..."[190]   that evokes controversy and hostility: "it were enough to entitle those Browne sectaries of the Blacke Prince, with the name of Traytors,"[191] although the term was used more generally and less harshly as a synonym for "disciple," as in "Aristotle...sending Calisthenes, a sectarie and kinsman of his, unto Alexander...."[192] If sectaries tend to blindly parrot the beliefs of their charismatic masters, e.g., "which Mahomet so strongly infused into his Sectaries,"[193] then they are possessed by "a kind of Sectary Passion"[194] that indicates intolerance of ideas and practices that contradict their own: "Sectary-metaphysicians...will, we fear be disappointed in our chapters on memory, imagination and judgment They will not find us partisans of any system."[195]

Sectaries, then, have beliefs and behaviors that indicate loyalty to their exclusive groups and masters, "the sectatours of Thessalus, that is, to wyt they that obserue his preceptes,"[196] and "He doth forbid al his sectatours Mahometistes to drinke wine."[197] Sect membership, then, implies a high level of conformity and some individuals unabashedly ape their leaders' words and deeds, "Those... which gaue themselves to follow and imitate others, were in all things so observant sectatours of those masters...."[198] Worshipping the master as the holy fountain of superior wisdom and virtue leads to the loss of moral autonomy and critical judgment, "Such markes as clearly showed him...to have been a Sectator of these great masters of Antiquity,"[199] and "they themselves are fanatic sectators of the old Koran reading."[200]

The votary [L: ppl. stem of vovere] is a person "bound by a vow; a devotee,"[20] such as monks and nuns discipled by their orders to engage in study, meditation and ritual practice in God's service: "monastaries of votaries under special and peculiar vows and rules"[202]; and the "votarie... will not cut his haire until the experation of his vow."[203] To reach a higher spiritual plane of pure devotion, the votary ideally sacrifices immediate pleasure and egoistic interest, accepting the authoritative commands of superiors believed to possess knowledge of how to achieve salvation and of what is best for the community, "I shall not be ashamed to own myself a Votary to all your commands,"[204] and "the Christ-like love all other loves exceed, by which to save a soul Christ's vot'ry bleeds."[205]

In figurative use, a votary is a disciple of a pagan divinity that inspires and confers benefits in return for faithful worship: "Hear, Goddess, hear thy votary. Thy nearest of thy sons inspire,"[206] and "Before the goddess' shrine we too, love's votaries bend."[207] Loosely used, any person is a votary when ardently devoted to a god, master, subject matter or an inanimate object, "Harold implored the help of the relic whose sworn votary he was,"[208] and "If philosophy befouls her votaries... let her be sent back to the infernal regions."[209] Loyal service brings rewards, "the boundless store of charms which nature to her votary yields,"[210] although bad things may follow when promises are not kept for reason of incomplete devotion or bad character, "I am a rejected votary at the shrine of health,"[211] and "science requires a certain inward heat and heroism in her votaries."[212] Also, a votary can be self-destructive for failing to see the negative features of its object of devotion, "He became... even a more devoted votarie to gambling than ever before,"[213] or "votaries of business and pleasure prove faithless alike in friendship and love."[214]

CHAPTER TWO

Aristotle and
the Nature of Knowledge

The Three Types of Masters

Having delineated the concepts of master and disciple, it is necessary to distinguish the types of masters, disciples and the different forms of their relationship. My claims are, following Aristotle, that knowledge can be broken down into three varieties (techne, phronesis and sophia); that three types of masters can be distinguished according to the forms of knowledge they claim to possess; that persons with particular intellectual, spiritual and practical goals are attracted to one or other genre of masters because they want to learn the knowledge they allege to offer; that the three types of masters have distinct self-understandings as educators, varied attitudes about the nature and goals of discipleship; and, as a consequence, the character and dynamics of their relationships with followers vary.

The three major species of knowledge Aristotle delineates have three correlative ideal-typical types of masters: master-artisans possess technical/craft knowledge (techne); masters of prudence claim insight into practical affairs (phronesis); and masters of wisdom affirm having metaphysical and moral truths gained from contemplation (sophia).

What general qualities distinguish each category of masters, and what implications follow from Aristotle's tripartite division of knowledge for conceiving of different forms of the master/disciple relationship? And do standards exist that enable potential disciples to judge whether a particular master is the real article or a fake?

The Master as Artisan

For Aristotle, the knowledge appropriate to the technical arts, whether shipbuilding, medicine, architecture, weaving, painting, tanning or sculpting, is that of making or producing (poiesis):

> The business of every art is to bring something into existence, and the practice of an art involves the study of how to bring into existence something which is capable of having such existence and has its efficient cause in the maker and not in itself, it follows that art, being a kind of making, cannot be a kind of doing.[1]

The master-artisan is skilled in a narrow domain and has technical control of the materials and procedures to achieve the goals for which his craft exists, whether the physician identifying symptoms and prescribing treatments to restore health, the shoemaker telling a client that his sandals are too old to be repaired at a reasonable price, or the violinist teasing his bow with consummate technique on perfectly tuned strings to make lovely sounds. Knowledge of the basic rules and methods of one art are not readily applicable to another, as the various arts have their own specific precepts, procedures and goals. For example, the principles governing the production of shoes are not helpful to a physician's treatment of a malignant growth, to the skillful playing of a piano, or to the art of safe sailing against strong winds.

Diverse forms of *techne*, then, are required by various arts to make things or produce desired conditions, and the master-artisan stands as a principle of efficient causality because he knows the fundamental principles of his art and the procedures to be employed to achieve projected results, whether fine tuning a musical instrument, mending a broken bone, or building a strong foundation for a house. The knowledge of technical principles and procedures that leads to firm control over materials and processes of production are grounded in experience which taught the master-artisan exactly what by nature is possible and impossible. For example, good shoemakers know that soles made of paper lack the strong, relatively enduring properties of rubber or leather, and that the latter two materials may be broken down into better and poorer grades that have their own subtle but specific traits. Identical or similar objects or conditions can be produced by using repetitive methods derived from sound principles, and contingencies and uncertainties can be greatly minimized, if not entirely eliminated, by a rational strategy of trial and error. Such is the nature of *techne*.

The Disciple as Apprentice

If the knowledge of master-artisans is narrow in scope and justifies itself by producing useful things or results, it follows that a student of the master is properly called an apprentice who through imitation (mimesis) learns the principles and methods governing a specialized craft. The apprentice naturally enters into a subordinate relationship to an authoritative person who wields power over him, judges his talents, temperament and suitability for a particular line of work, and who generally disciplines him when deemed necessary. Also, the basic rules and steps of craft-production can be codified and summarized for apprentices to learn, although abstract insight into principles are hardly substitutes for actual hands-on production guided by the superior model of the master who points out errors and makes corrections learned from extensive experience.

The master/apprentice relationship carries no built-in expectation that discipleship result. To the contrary, the apprentice under the master's watchful guidance may eventually become a journeyman and finally, after years of preparation, a master himself upon presentation of a Meisterwerk that proves attainment of levels of knowledge and technique that qualify him as an independent practitioner of the art. Yet discipleship may occur in the arts and crafts if the new Meister's work is largely imitative of his educator's methods and styles, identifying him as unoriginal and a member of certain master's school. Remaining an imitator compromises the spirit of independence and equality inherent in the ideal of completing a Meisterwerk—a work that should only be approved when marked by some originality and not because it pleases the master to have successfully "discipled" some of his favorite students.

Still, discipleship to a master-artisan would be quite narrow in scope and consequence, limited to principles and practices that pertain only to the sphere of the art itself. A master-artisan who claimed, on the basis of possessing a narrow techne, privileged insight into good and evil, how the soul is to be purified and saved, of what the best form of political association consists, the essential differences between illusion and reality, or which foods are truly best for a healthy body, would be stating mere opinions to his students who want to learn his craft to find employment, not to hear his ramblings about obscure matters for which craft-knowledge cannot be a guide or their master an authority.

Persons claiming to be master-artisans who possess techne can easily be falsified if they are liars. For example, if I take my worn sandals needful of soles and heels to the new shoemaker located on mainstreet, then his technical skill is tested by the quality of the repair. If the fixed sandals rapidly wear out or fall apart, there would be strong grounds for judging him a poor artisan who uses inferior materials, a perception validated by the experience of my neighbors who also complained to me about his shoddy work—excellent grounds for thinking him an incompetent dolt and certainly no master. And his three apprentices would likely not remain with him long after hearing customer complaints and noticing the serious loss of business, recognizing that learning the craft of shoe repair from him would be a gross mistake.

The Master of Political Prudence

Politics for Aristotle is decidedly not a techne concerned with making or producing according to relatively invariant principles but an activity belonging to the sphere of what by nature is conditional and change-able. The knowledge appropriate to action is phronesis which is inherently imprecise and subject to the disconcerting effects of the contingent and the unforeseen. Even the best master-politician may fail to build a winning coalition, gauge the mood of the citizens at a crucial point of decision, correctly predict the machinations of rivals, or adequately assess the exact amount of resources required to realize a particular goal. Compared to the success of the master-artisan who nearly always achieves predictable, repetitive results, the master-politician finds it much more difficult to control outcomes, largely because politics is, as Aristotle contends, a sphere marked by the uncertainties of deliberation and action:

> Deliberation is concerned with things
> which, while in general following certain
> definite lines, have no predictable issues,
> or the result of which cannot be clearly
> stated, or in which, when important
> decisions have to be made, we take
> others into our counsels, distrusting
> our own ability to settle the point.[2]

Politics naturally involves deliberation or forethought, and that entails judging the significance of events and changes in social and economic conditions that impact the well-being of the community, as the prelude to taking specific actions intended to actualize values or conditions that deliberation deems desirable, usually through the implementation of general policies and specific legislation. However, there is no guarantee of success because even the most astute deliberation may not foresee contingencies or correctly evaluate current forces, facts and events in the empirical world. Politics, then, is about action, not making or producing, and involves persons striving to realize their particular purposes, interests and ethical aims in a universe of clashing wills.

The master-politician fully realizes that persuasion or subtle manipulation of others is necessary to gain his ends, and further, that the resistance encountered when deliberating and acting is of a different nature than that experienced by the master-artisan who relies on techne to overcome the intractability of inert matter in making a useful object. The master-politician marked by high rates of success has available a storehouse of experience from acting in a multitude of situations that taught him prudence—the supreme political excellence—and in addition, has a large dose of favorable fortuna, that enigmatic and unforeseen ruler of human affairs which bestows its curses and blessings with a will of its own. However, the traits needed for political excellence might be judged, from the standpoint of the philosopher who possesses sophia, to be of lower rank than moral virtue or even its opposite. For Aristotle, political excellence cannot be defined according to some eternally stable standard, as empirical observation shows the traits that constitute "excellent" and "good" citizenship in one regime are sometimes entirely different, or even opposed, to those judged worthy of fine citizens in another. Acting well in politics requires prudence, the ability to make the most fitting choices in a complex universe of conflicting forces, moral dilemmas, and needful compromises. The master-politician achieves power and success despite the inherent fragility and transience of political life and, above all, recognizes that successful past choices may prove poor guides to the future, for acting well is dependent on astute evaluations of the possibilities inherent in particular contexts and not on the rigid application of universal rules of techne.

The Disciple as Political Actor

Master-politicians would, given their claim to possess prudential knowledge, attract disciples of a different character than persons apprenticing themselves to master-artisans. An individual with a strong record of success in public affairs would be a magnet for those wanting to accumulate and hold power, techniques for fending off rivals, and rules for manipulating complex situations for political advantage—assuming of course that a master-politician desired disciples and could be persuaded to release the secrets of his art given the possibility these might be used against him. Further, it is quite uncertain that a master's accumulated political experience could be codified into abstract rules teachable to others because acting well in politics is much less predictable, given its inherent novelties and situational diversities, than engaging in production or making that follows relatively invariant procedures.

Let me dig more deeply. The master-politician who attracted disciples would try to distill maxims for political success from his own experience and ask them to learn these. Besides having to fathom the exact meanings of the maxims through study and discussion without having much background experience of their own to guide them, the disciples would have to judge which specific political situations they encounter are truly similar to those described by their masters before proceeding to act. Obviously the room for error is great. The disciples might perceive false analogies, act on these, and fail as a result; and repeated failure might persuade them that the master's maxims are not very helpful because political events and situations never recur in exactly similar forms to permit standardized maxims to be routinely applied, revealing that the constellation of forces that account for successful [not necessarily ethical] actions are inherently obscure. In short, successful experience in politics might be an indeterminate blend of rational, intuitive and chance elements. Some disciples would likely become frustrated and conclude that political actors have different experiences, and may learn opposite lessons, in roughly similar situations. Success at politics, then, cannot be codified into a universally valid recipe book of rules, and further, foresight and uncanny intuition cannot be easily taught, if at all.

Discipleship to masters of political prudence is inherently weak and without staying power, for lacking a record of helping disciples succeed, such masters could hardly found schools to attract followers to provide commentary on, and dissemination of, their practical knowledge. Two of the greatest masters of political insight, Thucydides and Machiavelli, neither had disciples in the strong sense of Plato, Aristotle or Hegel, nor sought to found schools, likely realizing that their teachings promised no certainty in helping others achieve fame, power and glory in a political world where forces, events and persons are in constant flux.

Thucydides and Machiavelli are masters of prudential knowledge who recorded insights about politics gained from their rich political experience and astute reflection. They share some common assumptions, including: that the play of politics is universally driven by the motives of fear, honor and interest; that moral claims made by political actors often mask and rationalize the quest for power; that even the best planned policies and actions can fail given the presence of fortuna in human affairs; and that history moves in repetitive cycles, causing political events, situations and types of action to occur in analogous forms. Also, neither offered systematic theoretical arguments to justify their observations about human nature and politics nor adequately showed that they actually distilled their own political experiences and readings of history into prudential maxims that could be taught and successfully practiced. Perhaps Thucydides and Machiavelli failed to found schools to attract disciples because they recognized their inability to promise certain knowledge about the rules governing the gaining and holding of political power, let alone wisdom about cosmic things, the perfection of moral character, or how the power struggles, deceptions and violence of politics might be transcended. I cannot imagine that persons wanting knowledge from masters of prudence—assuming they could be found and that prudence is teachable—would feel strong bonds of love and community toward them, for their aims are neither friendship nor the search for truth but the gaining of instrumental knowledge to further political goals.

Finally, the master/disciple relationship built on the teaching and learning of phronesis is rather superficial and narrow in scope. The master-politician neither claims wisdom about cosmic issues, such as why all things come into being only to pass away, what happens to the soul after death, or of what good and evil consist, nor offers original insights into the nature of a well-ordered and just society, into the perfection of moral character, or into the true sources of human happiness. Prudential knowledge, then, is at best helpful for learning some imprecise lessons about the ways of the world, its power struggles, deceptions and possibilities, for the purpose of aiding survival and promoting the realization of personal values and civic goals in contexts of clashing wills and inherent limits. The master of prudence offers no hope of transforming the political world to end its inherent violence, deceptions and conflicts, and there is no special vision of personal or communal salvation and perfection. Finally, his disciples feel no particular bonds of love, gratitude and community toward him, at least in the manner found among disciples of Jesus or Buddha, with whom they formed life-long, unbreakable relationships that sometimes involved great personal sacrifices.

The Master of Sophia

Aristotle says of the contemplative life:

> For contemplation is the highest
> form of activity, since the intellect is

the highest thing in us. It will not
be lived by us in our merely human
capacity but in virtue of something
divine within us, and so far as this
divine particle is superior to man's
composite nature, to that extent will
its activity be superior to other forms
of excellence.[3]

Sophia, or wisdom, is what the philosopher ideally possesses, and the striving to gain it grows from a
deep experience of wonder at having mind and life, at
possessing the dual identity of being an individual and
social creature, and at dwelling in a cosmos populated
with a rich diversity of forms, whether inorganic, sen-
sate or spiritual. The philosopher is perplexed at who
and what we are, why we exist at all, where we are
going and, for Aristotle, has the leisure to contemplate the timeless archetypes in which all beings find
their ground of identity. The goal is to live in harmony with the rational plan manifest in God's creation, and that means ordering the parts of the *psyche*
so that reason, the highest and most divine aspect,
may not only govern the baser desires and turbulent
emotions, but is freed from transient concerns to become contemplative, that most sublime and beautiful
activity that gives lasting joy.

Intellectual contemplation that seeks imperishable,
eternal knowledge rests on a mental attitude radically

distinct from those of *techne* and *phronesis*. The philosopher neither seeks to produce useful material things to ease the burdens of everyday life, nor does he think that prudent action leading to political success is of the highest rank. Everything in life should be arranged to free reason from turbulence and distraction, for the philosopher ideally has neither ambitions for power, status or glory nor does he crave ordinary pleasures or luxuries, whether sexual, culinary or property, as the highest goals of existence. The attainment of *sophia*, then, signals metaphysical insight into the mainsprings of reality; however, such wisdom is rare, the preserve of a few spirits who overcome passions and temptations that prevent the mind's eye from soaring to heavenly spheres. The philosopher has the virtue of temperance, knowing what is due each part of the *psyche* and of what the just character of their reciprocal relations consists.

Aristotle's master-philosopher is hardly concerned with telling his disciples how to be good, effective citizens in the public world—for the teaching of *sophia*, not prudence, is his aim, and wisdom cannot guide excellent deliberation and action in politics, a world hopelessly mired in illusion, ceaseless change, and conflict. Philosophers are in deep error if they teach their disciples that *sophia* can cure the illnesses of the body-politic since politics can neither be made philosophical, a mirror of the eternal forms of justice, virtue and beauty, nor can eternity be politicized as it transcends worldly, ordinary realms of experience. For Aristotle, Plato committed ultimate folly by teaching his disciples that philosophers alone should rule, a mistake derived from his blurring the distinction between contemplative wisdom and craft-knowledge, as if a special political *techne* could fashion the perfectly just society using blueprints and standards derived from contemplative reason. Further, it was wrong of Plato to tell his disciples to abhor as evil the conflicts and ambiguities of politics, for these must exist if deliberation, judgment and action are to occur and if humanity is to retain its natural diversity of political expressions and ways of life.

Aristotle's claim that philosophical contemplation is radically different from prudential knowledge and cannot, by nature, provide politics with standards and goals, need not be accepted as the final word. Indeed, theorists who attract disciples and found schools often allege possessing wisdom to transfigure the public world and the *psyches* of the citizens, that is, they claim to bridge the chasm between *sophia* and practical affairs.

Plato thought that metaphysical insight can give standards for shaping excellent political institutions, for giving citizens insight into the nature of good and evil, and for formulating the proper goals of civil association. For example, Plato held with Socrates that it is always harmful to the *psyche* to return evil for evil, thereby breaking mightily with the traditional Homeric moral ideal that the gods sanction it just and desirable to hurt one's enemies. Plato's teaching that it is best never to retaliate when harmed in some fit of anger is presumably a piece of wisdom derived from philosophical insight into the *logos*, not from subjective judgment or intuition. Further, possessing *sophia* shows that believing in the correctness of common sense moral precepts, established customs, or the opinions of the so-called wise sometimes leads to error.

Socrates and Plato are not the only masters of wisdom to object to Aristotle's sharp division between philosophy and politics. Sir Thomas More suffered deeply because of the chasm he saw between the ideal and the real, between Christian values and the actual course of the world, and he felt impelled to write *Utopia* to educate people to understand that moral evils, including private property, exploitation of the poor, and the greed of princes, might be abolished, or at least greatly lessened, by implementing a perfected political world founded on the truths of philosophical contemplation that wove wisdom and virtue into its fabric of life. Hobbes thought that the violent disorders of politics in civil war England derived from a failure of people to share common and clear definitions of justice, authority, freedom and equality. If political knowledge was modeled along the lines of a philosophical geometry, with its precise and unassailable definitions, then humankind might be redeemed from its civic strife and confusions. Hobbes, as Plato and More, claimed to possess a healing wisdom.

Closer to our age is Hegel who affirmed that political communities, with their diverse values, institutions, life-cycles and historical differences, could be understood only by recourse to an esoteric knowledge of God's cosmic plan—a God who uses political life as the medium to actualize his striving to achieve higher levels unity, self-consciousness and freedom in his odyssey through time. For Hegel, political problems are ultimately cosmic ones. Marx also claimed rare theoretical insight, thinking he fathomed the materialist laws governing the creation and destruction of historical epochs, indeed, laws that determined their typical forms of culture, political ideologies, and patterns of consciousness, class and power. Thinking that he discerned the normally hidden forces from which capitalism grew, he took delight in explaining the secrets of its industrial might and endless technical innovation. Further, he offered hope to the downtrodden, exploited workers by promising them relief from their miseries, claiming that capitalism must inexorably negate itself owing to dialectical laws of contradiction that would lead the proletariat to arise from their alienated condition to take power from their oppressors and create a communist future of material abundance and human fulfillment.

Nietzsche also claimed a god-like wisdom, thinking that he alone diagnosed why Western civilization was experiencing a dangerous nihilistic crisis in its fabric of life, indeed, a crisis born of the failure of the highest values of the Socratic-Platonic and Christian traditions to provide healthy foundations for political and personal life, leading instead to the malformation of the human being and the loss of its natural potentials. He thought that age-old philosophical/moral concepts that distinguished between a timeless, perfect world of unity and being, and a lower, flawed one of suffering, multiplicity and temporality, resulted in life being experienced as impoverished, unworthy and needful of escape. Nietzsche, then, experienced himself as a "fatality" because he claimed the *sophia* to unlock the secrets of modernity's decadence and to offer humanity new values by which it might overcome its nihilistic "great weariness" to achieve the "great health."

Clearly, many masters of wisdom reject Aristotle's claim that prudential knowledge alone is appropriate to political affairs, and further, it is no accident that thinkers who affirm that philosophical discernment ought to fashion political affairs have throughout history attracted disciples and founded schools.

The Disciple as Seeker of Wisdom

Given Aristotle's conception of philosophy, the master of *sophia* would clearly attract disciples with different traits of mind and goals than found among followers of the master-artisan and master-politician. Discipleship would be an attractive option for persons wanting to perfect the moral virtues, to discipline their reason to contemplate eternal things, and to find spiritual fulfillment and abiding happiness through living rational and temperate lives. The master-philosopher, then, claims to possess *sophia* about the most obscure things, and further, may bridge the chasm between reason that articulates reality through concepts and a mysticism which silently experiences a union beyond linguistic representation. Disciples of the master of *sophia* would expect to gain purpose, centeredness and abiding happiness through learning to contemplate the mysteries of the imperishable order of being; and they would tend to gather into a small community, or form a cult, insulated from the ordinary distractions of life, where the master teaches them a special wisdom to purge their souls of the unwholesome effects of the baser passions and to recognize their divine nature.[4]

Under their master's guidance, whom the disciples experience as powerfully charismatic and a shining example of the highest moral and intellectual virtue, they see themselves as initiates into a rare wisdom from which the run of humanity is disbarred—a perception that may lead them to exude airs of self-indulgent vanity and superiority. And the master's antipathy to power, status and wealth as dangers to the psyche—assuming he is not a hypocrite who separates word from deed—is perceived by them as living proof of his difference not only from ordinary people but from rival philosophers and religious teachers whom the master sometimes portrays to his disciples as seductive sophists offering false wisdom.

Given the potential to induce deep transformations in his disciples, the master of *sophia* can become a pater familias who enters into emotionally charged relationships with his followers whom he may treat as dependent children, demanding from them obedience, positive reinforcement when he voices his prejudices, opinions, loves and hates, and may even cultivate blind hero worship of his person. For their part, the disciples may compete for their master's attention and affection, show jealousy when he picks favorites, feel guilt when they fail to meet his expectations, and develop powerful emotional and intellectual identifications with him that can result in imitative behaviors that last their whole lifetimes and even after the master's death.

CHAPTER THREE

The Transmission of Knowledge

Theoretical Education

The learning process that some persons receive from charismatic masters of wisdom which leads their ceasing to be ordinary students to become disciples and adherents I call theoretical education—a form of education that should be separated from a less transformative type of digesting knowledge, namely, that of being intellectually influenced. One can absorb a good deal from a teacher without becoming a disciple whose intellectual and emotional identity is tied to the person and doctrine of another. Theoretical education involves the master, or his chief followers, socializing persons to be adherents of a teaching that entwines with their intellectual and emotional identities, and further, is often accompanied by the disciples congregating together in schools, sects or cults of like-minded "friends" to provide mutual support and reinforcement for their shared ideas that mark themselves as different from "outsiders" who are not party to their special wisdom. Theoretical education, then, is a process of "discipling" wherein persons learn rich languages composed of conceptual distinctions, moral precepts, civic agendas, and habits of observing, describing and understanding reality. Disciples also learn what things and persons are worthy of acceptance, rejection, love, and hate, and about what precepts of conduct, faith and belief are appropriate to their membership in a community.

What makes theoretical education possible by masters of wisdom is that they are inevitably persons with striking traits of character, unusual intellects, powerful convictions, passionate visions, and claim missions—contrary to Aristotle's warnings—to diagnose and heal the disorders they claim exist in the public world and in individual psyches. Magnetic qualities of masters pull relatively unformed youths into their orbits of influence; after all, youths especially seek clarity about their own identities, take the tragedies and paradoxes of life to heart, are susceptible to an untamed wondrous exuberance, and are attracted to ideas that promise them wholeness and the end to confusion and discontent. Masters who teach others rich symbolic worlds that give sense to bewildering facts and events, and that offer a path to a healing knowledge, must appeal to persons uncertain of their own abilities and powers.

For their part, masters of wisdom engage in

discipling for several reasons: to ensure their teachings are codified, enriched and transmitted to future generations; to be defended against the attacks of detractors; to be surrounded by worshipful persons who validate their ideas and persons; to have their theories, civic agendas and ethical precepts impact on the public world; and to satisfy their drive to circumvent oblivion after their deaths by having their ideas and deeds live in the memory of others. Of course having disciples can pose dangers to masters, including misinterpreting doctrine or willfully distorting it for self-serving reasons; and masters may try to protect themselves by dividing disciples into distinct types judged to have more or less desirable qualities of mind and character, some of whom are introduced to the deepest levels of doctrine whereas others are purposely taught at a superficial level to keep potential harm to a minimum.

Disciples may also suffer from their attachment to charismatic masters, including the loss of critical intellectual capacity and emotional self-sufficiency; moral corruption and abject dependence on the powerful for survival; wrongful idealization of the master as heroic and virtuous; rejection of rival teachers and their adherents without sufficient reason; and the fragmentation of disciples into disputatious factions after the master's death leading former friends into rivalry and conflict. Further, the allegiance of disciples to a master of wisdom inevitably involves a leap of faith because of the absence of objective criteria to establish indisputably clear boundaries between true and false teachers. A danger is that the master may be no true master at all, but a sophisticated charlatan adept at attracting followers and exploiting their awe, affection, trust and lack of critical distance to further his own personal and intellectual agendas, including creating an exclusive cult or school populated by epigoni who think their highest duty in life is to be partisans on behalf of his person and "true" teaching.

There are at least three forms of discipleship in the history of political theory, of which two, the disciple-become-master and the creative revisionist, are healthy expressions whereas I judge the epigone, the third and currently most pervasive form, to have some destructive elements.

In the course of passing generations a rare and supremely powerful event occurs, namely, the creation of a new theory from an older one. The overall pattern is deceptively simple: an especially gifted disciple struggles with his master's concepts and values, and from that encounter, founds an original theory. Not unexpectedly, the new theory shows some family resemblances to the one from which it grew, retaining from it recognizable questions, problems, ideas, and modes of analysis. However, these resemblances are ultimately overshadowed because the former disciple has not merely revised a theory, but given birth to a new paradigm of thought. What occurs, then, is an Aufhebung, a movement of consciousness that cancels out what previously existed while preserving some of its elements in a radically transfigured form. Disciples who become masters clearly possess imaginative genius and a powerful need to be spiritually and intellectually independent.

Plato, Aristotle, Marx and Nietzsche strike me as examples of theorists who began their vocations as disciples only eventually to become masters, and each reveals a unique way of travelling that path. They shared the experience of receiving formative educations from seminal thinkers before fully finding their own creative voices; and further, their respective mature ideas maintain some strong family resemblances to those of their teachers.

The imaginative vision of the perfectly just society of the Republic, with its anti-democratic spirit and passion for order, its rule by wise philosophers who discern eternal Ideas to provide models for fashioning virtuous institutions and temperate psyches, and its focus on the principles of excellent education, are fruitfully understood as creative transformations of concepts that Plato learned from Socrates. Plato's theorizing about the dialectic as the best method of finding stable, universal definitions of moral terms; about the intrinsic rewards of living according to standards dictated by reason; and about how the good person should never retaliate for an injury done to him by another, as that would malform his own soul—all evolved from his learning experiences with Socrates. Plato's using Socrates' figure as the leading speaker in the majority of his dialogues—a Socrates made eternally young and vital—testifies to his teacher's lasting impact on him.

The roughly twenty years Aristotle studied with Plato in the Academy, where he learned to theorize by writing dialogues modeled on those of his teacher, provided him with the essential moral and intellectual paradigms that he eventually addressed in achieving his original voice. Still, the determination of Aristotle to walk his own path cannot hide the fact that his Politics reveals significant affinities to Plato's Laws, and that basic features of his metaphysical, ethical and even physical theories took shape in the activity of rethinking complex ideas he learned from his master. The mature works of Aristotle frequently and pointedly address and correct Plato's theories in the context of the former disciple formulating his own creative solutions to issues that also troubled Plato. Aristotle declared his independence from and challenged his great educator by founding the Lyceum to surpass in wisdom Plato's school, the Academy.

Marx lacked a personal relationship with Hegel, his most significant teacher, but that hardly prevented him as a young man from fully absorbing Hegel's rich conceptual world by avidly reading his texts, and by participating in the debates raging among the master's left-wing and right-wing disciples about how to interpret, and apply to politics, his challenging if ambiguous theories of the state, history, dialectics, and alienation. The young Marx might be called a disciple-at-a-distance because, lacking a personal relationship to Hegel, he absorbed his teachings directly from texts and from followers who claimed privileged insight in the master's concepts. Marx found his own creative voice through a process of subjecting Hegel to basic criticism, and perhaps deceived himself by not fully admitting that his own methods of analysis, accounts of historical development, and critiques of civil society, retained strong family resemblances to Hegel's thinking.

Nietzsche was unique because he was discipled by two masters, Schopenhauer and Wagner. He learned from Schopenhauer philosophical pessimism, an aristocratic conception of the theoretical life, unique views about art, music, tragedy, the will-to-live, and antipathy toward historicism, rationalism, and doctrines of progress. From his intense relationship with Wagner, he came to judge European culture as a wasteland in need of renewal; and further, the Maestro taught him to idealize ancient Hellenic tragedy as the medium through which citizens were educated to harmonize their conflicting passions and to give meta-physical meaning to suffering. As Nietzsche developed, his hero-worship of Schopenhauer and Wagner was replaced with critical comments about their theories, and his own mature philosophy can be viewed profit-ably as transfigurations of ideas he learned from them.

My claim, then, is that detailed studies of the pe-riods of discipleship of Plato, Aristotle, Marx, and Nietzsche would help illuminate the nature of the in-tellectual processes, and emotional and interpersonal dynamics, by which their mature theories grew from the ones they learned from great masters. In short, each underwent the distinctive experience of receiv-ing a theoretical education, a concept that promises a rich way to understand the genesis of new theories from older ones in cases where the master/disciple relationship is a formative, powerful and abiding event. Of course not every master/disciple relationship leads to the transfiguration of the old into the new, as most who follow the theories of others never transcend the discipleship role.

Let me be crystal-clear to avoid confusion! I am not claiming that every great political theorist began as a disciple, nor that every new theory is primarily generated from a struggle of a highly gifted disciple against the ideas of his master. For example, it would be foolish to explain the origins of the mature theo-ries of Hobbes, Locke, and Rousseau in terms of my idea of theoretical education, if only because they never were disciples of great masters who provided them with personal experiences and powerful concepts that they eventually transfigured. Great intellect, moral passion, the drive to think against the grain, the rare ability to look at the familiar in new and striking ways, and the ideational influences of other thinkers, when combined with a feeling for crisis in culture and society, constitute the major forces that explain the genesis and evolution of most political theories. Nevertheless, the drive of the disciple to achieve intellectual and emotional independence from the master can be a significant, even a determining, factor.

Intellectual Influence

Still, the reader might reject my suggestion that the dynamics of master/disciple relationships can, in selected cases, be decisive for understanding how and why new theories grow from older ones, and proceed to counsel me: "Dear Hal Sarf, just drop the categories of theoretical education and disciple-become-master and simply trace the flow of 'influence' from one thinker to another, paying close attention to the specific ideational elements the recipient thinker borrowed and perhaps transformed. After all, excellent cases can be made that Plato, Aristotle, Marx and

Nietzsche owed as much or more to thinkers other than the ones you called their 'theoretical educators.'" Let us test the merits of such well-meant advice.

Perhaps key concepts of Plato's philosophy are more indebted to the influences of Parmenides and Pythagoras than to Socrates. Surely we discern the guiding light of Parmenides in Plato's teaching that eternal Ideas are the ultimate reality and the only true object of philosophical reflection; and that sense-experience must reveal illusions and instabilities, providing no secure foundation for knowledge. Further, did not Pythagoras profoundly influence Plato's conception that the soul transmigrates upon death; that a correct understanding of mathematical numbers and musical harmonic scales can educate the soul to balance its conflictual elements; and that philosophy is an esoteric activity accessible to a few initiates who must purify themselves before receiving special wisdom? Why the insistence, then, that Socrates was Plato's theoretical-educator?

Similarly, cannot a strong case be made that Feuerbach's impact on Marx was greater than Hegel's because Feuerbach taught him a philosophical anthropology and method of transformational criticism that enabled Marx to expose Hegel as a mystical idealist? Can we justly deny the importance of Locke's labor theory of value for understanding Marx's own, or the impact of the economic ideas of Smith, Ricardo and

Malthus in shaping Marx's theorizing about the forces governing capitalist accumulation, investment and production? Would it not be downright silly to trace Marx's socialist values to Hegel? And why point to the central importance of Schopenhauer and Wagner on Nietzsche's development when some of his key ideas on culture, Greek tragedy, nihilism and the philo-sophical life can be better understood as stamped with the influences of Goethe, Schiller, Hölderlin, Montaigne, Emerson, Chamfort, Fontennele and the pre-Socratics, particularly Heraclitus?

Are these observations and refutations persuasive? Should I abandon exploring the genesis of new theo-ries from older ones from the perspective of the mas-ter/disciple relationship in cases where such a rela-tionship is powerfully present, and spend time more productively engaging in the traditional activity of searching for instances of intellectual influence? The answer is no!

The search for intellectual influences on a great thinker is certainly a normal activity for the historian of ideas. After all, no master-theorist creates concepts ex-nihilo from his own depths, unaffected by the cul-tural climate of his age or by the specific ideas of think-ers with whom he is familiar. However, establishing instances of the flow of "influence" from one thinker to another involves serious difficulties. Clear proof must be given that a borrowing of ideas actually took place, and further, that the event was truly significant. The establishing of intellectual influence, then, involves detective work; and the obvious danger is that misleading or superficial accounts may be given about the exact impact of one theorist on another.

For example, a plausible case is made that Marx's account of human beings as typically egoistic and aggressively conflictual in capitalism reveals the influence of Hegel's descriptions of life in civil society found in the Philosophy of Right. But has "influence" been actually established? Would it not be equally compelling to argue that Marx's views of human behavior in capitalism were less influenced by Hegel than by the writings of the British political-economists? And should we forget Proudhon, the early Russian anarchists and the French Utopian socialists? Perhaps they shaped Marx's outlook more than the others. Clearly, the search for "influence" easily leads the investigator into a mire; he is forced to compile unwieldy lists of thinkers as likely "sources" for a particular theorist's ideas, and then must decide which of the candidates are "more" or "less" influential and in what exact respects—often with the result of much quibbling and little illumination.

If real problems are met trying to visualize the flow of influence of even a single idea from one thinker to another, then imagine the problems encountered if the goal is to understand the origin, evolution and paradigmatic features of theories whose creators were marked by phases of discipleship to great masters. For instance, to know that Nietzsche's theory of tragedy borrowed a few specific ideas from Schiller or Goethe fails to explain the genesis and general identity of the thought-forms to which these specific "borrowed" ideas were melded. This is the point where the concept of theoretical education becomes decisive.

Examining Nietzsche's phase of discipleship to Schopenhauer and Wagner would illuminate the nature of the concepts and values he learned from them that shaped his basic modes of thinking about metaphysics, music, and Greek tragedy. Then we could accurately perceive how Nietzsche utilized particular ideas from Schiller and Goethe to buttress and deepen an already existing theoretical paradigm he learned from his two true educators. Clearly, Schiller and Goethe influenced Nietzsche; but they neither taught him fundamental concepts and values that he transfigured in achieving his own mastery, nor do they stand as central figures that he addresses and criticizes in his mature phase of thinking—which is the case with Schopenhauer and Wagner. Being theoretically educated is not the same as being merely influenced; the former involves a richer, more lasting form of learning than the latter.

Nietzsche could borrow ideas from Schiller and Goethe without becoming their disciple; and the same holds true for Plato's using Parmenidean and Pythagorean ideas, or Marx assimilating some concepts from Locke and Proudhon. These disciples-become-masters simply took what they needed from influential thinkers to enrich and ultimately transfigure the theoretical educations that formed their early intellectual identities—the learning experiences they received from their true master-educators.

The disciple-become-master, then, initially learns a conceptual universe comprised of complex meanings that must be illuminated, criticized and reworked in the process of founding a new theory. The new master-theory inevitably reveals family resemblances to the older one because the disciple finds his own path by a process of rethinking traditions of theorizing that once gave him intellectual identity. Traditions are never entirely erased by the disciple-become-master; instead, older thought forms and ideals are transfigured and expressed in new guises. We have identity and difference!

Discipleship, then, involves the learning totalities or gestalts that contain complex meanings and ways of thinking that cannot be fully understood in terms of examining the individual parts of which they are composed. The whole precedes and shapes how its constituent elements are organized, expressed, and given identity. A disciple, then, armed with his master's theoretical paradigm, much of which is tacit and not

easily articulated, may take x and y ideas from another thinker —"be influenced"—and alter these to
"fit" into his world-view in a fashion that retains little
resemblance to the original form and identity of the
ideas. To be influenced, then, neither carries any imperative to accept the connections between ideas as
understood by the "influencer," nor must the "influenced" thinker embrace the ethical aims, personal intentions and emotional tones that the "influential"
theorist associated with his concepts.

CHAPTER FOUR

The Master as Savior

Philosophers and Gurus

Masters of wisdom may be separated into two ideal types, namely, the philosopher and the guru. Although both have charisma and the drive to have disciples and to educate them, they differ because the philosopher as a pure type claims knowledge is achieved through the power of reason to penetrate reality and to articulate it through rich concepts communicable to others whereas the guru affirms that insight about ultimate things is found through dwelling directly in these, an experience that cannot be shared directly or fully represented in abstract ideas, but only evoked through disciplines, exercises and evocative images that help disciples pass beyond the boundaries of language to the "other side." Of course the two ideal types are not always mutually exclusive as a particular master may combine features of both in his own person in different weights and degrees, as witnessed by Plato's Socrates who ascends to the sun of knowledge to gaze speechless into a glorious radiance that disables the intellect's power to articulate that silently powerful experience, but only to recover and reluctantly descend again to that shadowy cave of perpetual illusion to describe in metaphor and allegory to the ignorant the nature of that previously inexpressible moment of dwelling in the white light of perfect insight.

The philosopher as a master of wisdom originates in ancient Greek discourse about the power of reason to discern the lineaments of the cosmic and human orders; about the purgation of evils from the psyche and its salvation; about the boundaries between knowledge, belief and opinion; about the differences between exoteric and esoteric presentations of truth; about the qualities that distinguish the enlightened and noble soul from the ignorant and base one; about the meanings of happiness, virtue, justice and temperance, as well as their opposites, including evil, vice, cowardice, disorder and violence; and about how the polis is to weave justice into its fabric and provide paideia and excellent statesmanship for its citizens.

Philosophers from Pythagoras and the pre-Socratics through Plato, the atomists and the early Stoa to Epicurus, the Cynics, Skeptics and Epictetus, were neither as determined in the manner of Aristotle to classify the vast panorama of knowledge into distinct disciplines nor to identify philosophy exclusively with a particular subject matter, whether cosmology, ethics, politics, epistemology, or ontology. Instead, the impulse was for philosophy to cross artificial boundaries and to weave fields of knowledge into a totality of organic, interpenetrating parts, as witnessed most powerfully in Plato whose ideal state is fashioned under the influence of several sources, including Parmenides' ontological vision of a timeless order of Being, Orphic ideas of the purification and transmigration of the soul, Socrates' faith that universal, stable definitions of moral terms exist to establish standards to separate knowledge from opinion with regard to good and bad conduct, Pythagoras' concept that happiness is founded by harmonizing tensional elements within the soul, and Aeschylus and Sophocles who taught that the universe in which human life is imbedded is a moral order that when violated results in terrible punishments to both the individual and the state.

The tradition of Greek philosophy from Pythagoras through the Stoics and Epicureans of the Hellenistic period find thinkers of diverse theoretical orientations addressing some common issues that bridge religion and philosophy in languages that are suggestively metaphorical and also analytic. Masters of wisdom theorized how happiness and centeredness can be gained in a world that often shows itself hostile to human desires and purposes; inquired into the sources of virtue and vice in the psyche; speculated about how reason could attune to the order of the cosmos to find joyful fulfillment; theorized about the qualities of mind and character that separate the wise from the ignorant; wondered how persons should reconcile their public and private lives and respond to the claims of the political order; philosophized about the nature of knowledge and the limits and possibilities of achieving it; and finally, stated the conditions and practices that would purify the soul of evils and illusions while preparing it for salvation.

Masters of wisdom, whether Pythagoras, Parmenides, Zeno, Plato, Epicurus or Epictetus, while drawing no absolute division between the impulses of philosophy and religion, affirmed the superiority of reason, thinking that it alone can discern the boundaries between good and evil and articulate the nature of abiding happiness. All sought disciples and founded schools or cults on the suppositions that their knowledge is rationally teachable to them, that the problems, perplexities and obscurities of life can be fathomed, and that the wounded spirit can be healed and made whole through *sophia*. The master is a bridge over which cross the truths of a higher world to the lower one of error and illusion; and his disciples may, through earnest identification and study with him, gain ultimate insight to end their confusion.

Jesus

The Greek term *didaskein*, "to teach, inform, instruct, demonstrate, prescribe,"[1] also denotes the "idea of repeatedly extending the hand for acceptance... causing someone to accept something."[2] However, Jesus neither is an ordinary *didaskalos* (teacher) who conveys simple facts, opinions and technical skills to students nor a philosopher who teaches his followers a wisdom gained through the disciplined use of reason, for his Jewish identity places him in a culture where the highest goal of life is to live in harmony with the dictates of the one almighty God by keeping his covenant and laws. The Hebrew terms, *yada* (cause to know, teach) and *yarah* (teach, instruct) are not primarily secular terms that denote "the communication of knowledge and skills, but refer to instruction in how to live, the subject matter being the will of God."[3] In Rabbinic Judaism, the rabbi is a teacher who interprets the rules and regulations of the Torah, the embodiment of God's will for his chosen community, and applies these concretely to perplexing or conflictual daily situations that require interpretation and adjudication, for the failure to follow the Law invites severe punishment from the Lord, a punishment that is often imposed on the whole community.[4]

Although Jesus as a master/teacher shared certain similarities to the traditional rabbi—and sometimes his disciples addressed him by that title—including teaching in synagogues and the Temple, engaging in doctrinal disputes over the Torah, reciting and interpreting scripture to his disciples,[5] it is abundantly clear that Jesus neither relied primarily on the Torah as his ultimate source of authority in rendering judgments about God's will, nor admonished people in the manner of the mainstream rabbinical tradition to follow the Law as their primary duty in life, clearly rejecting legalistic, formal obedience to rules as the sole foundation of a fulfilled life or as sufficient to establish a deep relationship to God. Unlike the rabbis, Jesus' followers saw him as the Son of God, the long expected *apostolos* and Messiah sent by his heavenly Father to proclaim the "glad tidings"—as the prophets foretold—of the imminent arrival of God's kingdom, and his teaching was decidedly unphilosophical, for he offered no systematic and abstract treatments of his major themes—sin, resurrection, grace, love, forgiveness, and the kingdom of light.

He urgently admonished people to repent their sins by transforming their spiritual and worldly lives, for his presence signified the eruption of the numinous Divine into the human order, soon to be followed by a final judgment day wherein the just and unjust will receive their due and be sent to final resting places of light and love or to darkness and death. Jesus, then, is the ultimate master-teacher who claims he alone knows the way to eternal life and salvation and can teach it to others. His words superseded established tradition, and his performing miracles, whether raising the dead, causing the blind to see, or curing lepers, when combined with great self-discipline in the face of temptations by Satan or the flesh, evidenced his divine nature and authority to his believers.

What did discipleship signify to Jesus given his claim to reveal ultimate mysteries to those with "ears to hear and eyes to see"? Jesus begins his mission of saving souls by calling a chosen few, the Twelve, to be witnesses, disciples and "fishers of men," and to walk behind him as the light of truth given him by the Father, for he is the "Lord of the harvest" who sends his disciples to gather the "lost sheep" of Israel into the community of God.[6] The Twelve are educated by the Master into esoteric secrets of the Kingdom; he endows them with powers to perform signs and miracles; and further, their evangelical activity to the errant, sick and poor carry his full authority as his spirit is the spring from which flows their words and deeds.[7] Discipleship to Jesus involves spiritual dying and rebirth, the shedding of an old life for a new one, and is made possible by personal contact with the Master who radiates fellowship and infinite love. Jesus, then, is marked by *charisma* to his disciples that far exceeds that of philosophical teachers, for he is the *Kyrios* or Lord who issues a commanding call to those he chooses to walk in his footsteps while rejecting others who would voluntarily join him because he judges they have flawed personal character, or, in the deep recesses of their hearts, are unable to enter into an unconditionally dependent relationship on him.[8]

Discipleship to the *Savior* means following him on the path he treads that alone leads to the heavenly Father, and that requires a total break with family, profession, residence and friends, for every attachment to the world must be rejected to enter into a consuming relationship with the "light, the way and the truth."[9] Only faith in him purifies the soul from sin and eases the burdens and sufferings of life; and, without his personal intercession, there is only annihilation and death—the lot of those who refuse his keys to the invisible kingdom given to him by the Father out of loving mercy. Total surrender to Jesus must last a lifetime, and that signifies disciples cannot expect to be masters in their own right or to have other teachers beside him, for he alone possesses divine wisdom and the power of grace.[10]

The unity of self with Jesus, and of the disciples with one another, creates a *corpus mysticum*, and, by emulating his way of life, a life illumed by the word of the Father, they conquer base desires, self-will and worldly ambitions to embrace humility, poverty and charity. The cost of discipleship to Jesus is high when judged by common standards of the good life, and even greater cost is possible because following him targets one for hostility, punishment and even death at the hands of those who reject his messiahship.[11] Serving Jesus means to share his cross of suffering, and that willingness indicates how faith in him effects a profound change in the heart that urges the will to risk everything to win eternal life by his side in the Kingdom of the Father.

The *charisma* of Jesus as a divine missionary was enhanced by his teaching through parables, for he thought that the truth is only accessible to those ready to receive it and will remain concealed to those un-ripe for his mysteries. Discipleship to the Master means a life of struggle to understand his parables about res-urrection, grace, love of neighbor, divine forgiveness, and the presence of God's Kingdom—parables being "graphic depictions of spiritual matters..." that recall the imagery of prophetic apocalypse.[12] Jesus must sometimes admonish and correct his followers' inad-equate perceptions of who he is, from whence he came, of what his words and actions consist, and of why suf-fering and self-sacrifice must be his inevitable lot.[13] Learning by listening to parables means transcending ordinary and philosophic reason as inadequate, for what he teaches cannot be articulated in abstract con-cepts or proven by ordinary empirical evidence, as the eye of the soul is forced to dwell directly in the truth after deep reflection on the riddles and striking images the parable contains. "Closer drew the Twelve disciples to their Master's side"[14] to listen carefully to his strange speech to gain insight into obscure but weighty matters; and using him as their supreme model, they strove to perfect their practice of life by befriending the despised, the weak and the sick, "why should I be ashamed of their company when my Master mingled with publicans and thieves?"[15] Because Jesus apparently wrote nothing, and because he spoke to crowds of people as he wandered from place to place, it was imperative that his remarks be condensed into memorable phrases and images, such as contained in parables, that hearers could easily retain after he left them.[16]

Being in discipleship to Jesus requires not only having faith in him but involves adhering to beliefs and practices that mark one as belonging to his spiritual body, "You are gathered here to take upon yourselves the obligations of Christ's disciples,"[17] and these include baptism, avoiding sin in thought and deed, loving thy enemy and turning the other cheek when provoked, and abolishing pride that creates the illusion of independence from the divine ground. Fulfilling the terms of discipleship cannot be met through empty gesture and ritual but must express the deepest, most heart-felt convictions of the soul, "if a true disciple, a true Christian; if but a formal disciple, surely but a hollow Christian."[18] The disciples experience themselves and life profoundly transfigured by the master's thamaturgical light of infinite love that binds all things together in the Father, "to the true disciple a miracle only manifests the power and love which are silently at work everywhere."[19]

Jesus clearly stands in a different relationship to his disciples than found among Greek philosophical teachers who, ideally, encouraged their followers to develop the rational element in the *psyche*, to explore the natures of virtue, happiness, temperance and justice, and to foster a capacity for independent critical judgment that might lead them to become their own masters. Unlike the philosopher who investigated the nature of the *logos* thought to permeate the whole of being, and to express its identity in conceptual form, Jesus claimed his wisdom was grounded in revelation given to him by the transcendent Father to transmit to humanity for its salvation. Jesus is a preacher of the path of righteousness who simultaneously moves within the horizons and language of traditional Hebraic law while revolutionizing its meaning and application, proclaiming the truth of God wherever he went and calling upon people to make life-transforming decisions to live in his image, thereby harmonizing their spirits with the divine plan, the precondition of wholeness and salvation. Ultimately Jesus is the supreme *Kyrios*, an imposing term of grandeur signifying that he is the Lord incarnate, and the judge who weighs the lives of others as to good and evil, deciding their salvation or damnation.

The Guru

To be human is to long for answers to perplexing questions about why we come into being only to pass away, about what ends ought to be pursued in the brief time allotted in our earthly sojourn, and about whether death signifies the absolute extinction of self or opens the door to another life. Enigmas about human fate and purpose lead people to turn to masters of wisdom who claim definitive answers to their questions about why life is suffering and how salvation is to be achieved. Jalal al-Din Rumi, a Sufi mystic, remarked that "Whoever travels without a guide needs 200 years for a two day journey,"[20] a sentiment echoed by spiritual masters of diverse traditions who judge that seekers of truth lacking careful instruction can make little progress on the road leading from ignorance to deliverance.

Religious masters, then, claim to have perfected themselves through direct experience of the sacred; have knowledge of the principles governing spiritual growth; and can help disciples in different stages of development remove obstacles to their illumination. If the highest spiritual insight could be achieved without the guidance of an authoritative teacher, we would have a case of a "masterless master" who taught himself the way to salvation solely by his own abilities and powers. But true illumination by oneself is difficult and rare, a fact that led Hui-neng, a renowned Chinese Ch'an master, to remark that the searcher will feel compelled to "obtain a good teacher to show him how to see into his own self-nature."[21]

The Hindu tradition endows the spiritual master with great status and power, making him the repository of esoteric, secret knowledge, and giving him a pivotal role in "discipling" persons willing to submit to his special mental and physical training to gain deliverance. The term *guru* literally means "weighty or heavy one" and is usually applied to the teacher of Yoga, a meditative practice that takes different forms but is always marked by an intense master/disciple relationship that may continue into future lives given the Hindu belief that souls not only reincarnate but that some relationships will recur according to Karmic laws.[22]

The guru is "weighty" and "heavy" because he possesses absolute insight into spiritual matters, and is etymologically connected to the Latin phrase *gravis auctor*—the significant or true authority who begins actions that others complete.[23] The *Adavaya-Taraka Upanishad* says the syllable *gu* signifies darkness; the syllable *ru* the destroyer of that darkness...," and hence he who "by reason of his power to destroy darkness...

is called the guru."[24]

The guru, then, is heir to the esoteric traditions of the *Upanishads* that promise knowledge of deliverance from suffering based on a metaphysical system in which the supreme Self, *Brahman*, is the sole reality and primordial cosmic force that spawns from itself the multiplicity of individuated beings—the unity that "never admits of duality under all the varieties and diversities of nature."[25] *Brahman* devolves into the phenomenal world of human beings as *Atman*, that part of us which is immortal because of its intrinsic oneness with the world-soul. The aim of human existence is deliverance from *Maya*, the plurality of appearances to which the self is enslaved by attachment to egoistic passions and worldly things as the only realities. The genuine guru who manifests purity, devotion and compassion is the guide who teaches his disciple that "Thou art this immortal, all pervasive, all Blissful Brahman. Thou art that—*Tat Tvam Asi*. Realize this and be free."[26]

The guru is hardly a perplexed person seeking the truth in the manner of a Socrates and rejects any notion that using reason to articulate ultimate reality in conceptual form leads to salvation. Reason is a vanity, a trap that seduces one into falsely believing that mind can penetrate the phenomenal world of illusions to what lay beyond; hence, reason only adds to the dangers, seductions and confusions that inhere in life.

The guru is enlightened through direct experience; he has arrived at his goal of oneness, "The guru is Brahman himself. He is an ocean of bliss, knowledge and mercy. He is the fountain of joy."[27] Dwelling in the immediacy of true reality signifies the guru has "raised himself from this to that [Maya to Brahman], and thus has a free and unhampered access into both realms" [the phenomenal and the noumenal].[28]

If the "guru is God himself manifesting in personal form to guide the aspirant,"[29] then according to the *Kundaly Upanishad*, he is the "helmsman who assists the pupil in crossing the ocean of phenomenal existence in the boat built from his knowledge," leading the disciple to "everlasting joy and infinite truth-consciousness."[30] As a realized being incarnating the divine, the guru's presence in the world of *Maya* is a gift of grace to disciples, and that grace is expressed through outward marks and signs that indicate a "change of being that spontaneously manifests itself to others, even to the natural environment."[31] What the guru says and does is the voice of God; indeed, "blind is the man who has not seen the divine master," and "without the Satguru no one ever found God, without the Satguru no one ever shall."[32]

What exactly does discipleship to the guru entail? *Guru-Bhakti*, or devotion to the master, stands at the center of most systems of yogic practice. The guru expects total obedience, love and reverence for reason that he commands esoteric knowledge of complex techniques of breathing, meditation and dietary rules necessary for spiritual development. His perfect selfhood flows from direct insight into ultimate reality, and his every command must be obeyed, for the "guru is God...a word from him is a word from God...,"[33] and in him "you have found your ideal of perfection... the pattern into which you wish to mould yourself."[34] The guru provides true insight into the holy scriptures that "are like a forest" of "ambiguous passages... which have esoteric meanings, diverse significance and hidden explanations" that cannot be fathomed by the ignorant.[35]

The road to salvation is marked by pitfalls and obstacles natural to the world of *Maya* and to the confused mind of the disciple; hence, it is necessary for the disciple to "live under a guru for the eradication of his evil qualities and defects,"[36] for "as a man cannot see his back, so also he cannot see his own errors."[37] For the disciple, the guru is akin to "armor and fortress" that guard him "against all temptations and unfavorable forces of the material world."[38] Without his guru, the disciple is a lost soul and vulnerable to demons and evils that shut the door to enlightenment, and the master alone "breaks the binding cords of attachment and releases the aspirant from the trammels of earthly existence."[39] The difficult climb to the heights of spiritual fulfillment is facilitated by meditating on the guru's image that embodies a transfigured state of being, and he can "transform the disciple by a look, a touch, a thought or a word...."[40]

The guru, then, bestows blessings on the disciple who worships his person, and the aspirant ought never to judge his master's words or deeds, no matter how strange or seemingly unjust, for "a true disciple is concerned only with the divine nature of the guru... the guru's action as a man is not the disciple's concern."[41] To achieve salvation requires the extinction of self, of ego-consciousness; only through tireless service to the guru can "the cancer of individuality be dissolved,"[42] and the more the guru is served "humbly, willingly, unquestioningly, unassumingly, ungrudgingly, untiringly and lovingly... the more divine energy will flow into you."[43]

As a continuous presence to the disciple's mind's eye, the guru immediately knows when the disciple's attention wanders from him and shirks his duties, for his uncanny insight into other spirits is not subject to limitations imposed by ordinary laws of space and time. Humility, meekness and utter devotion signal that the disciple vanquished his lower self and drinks "the spiritual nectar of immortality which flows from the Holy lips of the guru,"[44] and, above all, the "disciple who has faith in the guru argues not, thinks not, reasons not, cogitates not... he simply obeys, obeys and obeys."[45] The disciple must prove his merit by cleansing and purifying his soul of base desires and impulses, striving to "make himself a perfectly faultless piece of marble... to be carved and chiseled into the image of God" by the master.[46] Everything of true value is owed the guru by his disciple; he is truly blessed to find a "physician for the disease of *samsara*";[47] and it is only right to prostrate himself before the "life-saving feet of Satguru... worship the sacred feet of Satguru... meditate on the holy feet of Satguru... become the dust of the divine feet of Satguru."[48]

If the relationship between guru and disciple is life-transforming and unconditional, then the disciple invites punishment when he questions his master's legitimacy or frays their bond by speaking or acting in untoward ways. For example, doubting the guru's wisdom "is the greatest sin"; "disobedience to guru is digging your own grave"; "he who backbites his guru goes to the Rauraua Hell"; and "one who speaks indecently in the presence of the guru becomes a Brahma-Rakshasa (a formidable demon) in a waterless forest tract."[49] Penalties are particularly harsh in cases where the errant follower's guru had previously given "secret knowledge to his trusted disciple... after repeated entreaty and severe testing,"[50] but only to be later abandoned by him. Leaving the guru, then, can have horrific consequences in both the present and future lives: "May he who deserts his teacher meet with death. May he who discontinues the recitation of the mantra given to him by the teacher become poverty stricken. May he who deserts both teacher and mantra be cast into hell...."[51]

The *Mahabharata* says that the punishment for a disciple profaning the master's bedroom chamber is either self-castration or suicide by caressing a white-hot statue of a woman.[52] Unconditional discipleship, then, is an "either-or" affair in the Hindu yogic tradition; its rewards are potentially salvational and its penalties quite harsh. That stark alternative likely comes from attributing divinity and absolute power to the guru in spiritual and practical affairs, and from conceiving discipleship as total obedience, self-abnegation, and unquestioned service. However, a guru's authoritarian, even overtly harsh tyrannical behavior, is legitimated in the Yogic writings because he is the incarnation of God who possesses the power to "remove all your troubles, sorrows and obstacles... he makes you immortal and divine";[53] and further, "when God is angry, guru is the savior. When guru gets angry none is the saviour."[54]

If the true guru teaches liberation from *Maya* and the ego, and if he is truly the incarnation of *Brahman*, it follows that wanting wisdom from another source "is fruitless, weak and the cause of much affliction."[55] The problem is that persons wishing to disciple themselves must be able to discriminate between true and false gurus in an environment where many claim to

be enlightened beings, "Beware of these yogic charla-
tans, daylight dupes or posing gurus, black sheep who
are infectious parasites and burdens on society, who
are... vultures that prey upon the ignorant."[56] Choos-
ing a false guru jeapardizes the disciple's gaining liberation, "Oh Devi, there are many gurus on earth who
give what is other than the Self, but hard to find in all
the worlds is the guru who reveals the Self."[57] Aban-
doning oneself to a guru poses the danger of being exploited: materially by handing over money and posses-
sions to the guru; morally by obeying the guru's every
whim and providing free service; and spiritually by
being in discipleship to a sophistical master who has
not achieved enlightenment.

Of course matters are more complicated because
a guru who asks a disciple to make personal and material sacrifices might not always be a deceitful, self-
interested master. For example, the *Shiva-Samhita*
strongly urges that persons turn over their livestock
and property to the guru as conditions of discipleship
for reason that a wise master insists they renounce
worldly attachments as a test of their willingness to
lose their old selves to achieve total rebirth. Sacrifice
ought not to be confused with exploitation. Also, the
severe *Guru-Kula* system enjoins disciples to enter the
guru's household as obedient servants and dependent
children, for the guru "is one's father; the guru is one's
mother; the guru is God."[58]

Giving money and property to a reincarnated god to support his household is hardly a ground of complaint, for the disciple must do the unusual when judged by standards drawn from ordinary life. Still, false gurus exist and the more subtle of them are not easily discerned, as is the case with the devious pseudo-guru who, as part of his scheme to dominate others, says to the ignorant: "'Think for yourself. Do not surrender yourself to any guru...'"—a statement that really means "he intends to be the listeners' guru himself."[59] Still, the Hindu tradition affirms that the true guru is recognized by his ability to "clear your doubts...," and further, that if he is "free from greed, anger and lust... selfless, loving and I-less... you can take him as your guru."[60] The obvious problem is that an ignorant person willing to be "discipled" to gain liberation would hardly be able to tell whether a particular master "really" had these desirable qualities or only "appeared" to. A world filled with rival, disputatious gurus who denounce their competitors in wisdom and "where fighting is going on between different sects... and the disciples of one guru fight with the disciples of another guru in the streets and marketplaces,"[61] might suggest that a true guru is never a sectarian who lords over an exclusive cult, but dwells ego-less within the numinous joy of *Brahman*, that most universal energy to whom sects and other exclusivities are mere nothing.

CHAPTER FIVE

Epigones, Creative Revisionism, and the Disciple Become Master

CHAPTER FIVE

Epigones, Creative Revisionism,
and the
Disciple Become Master

The Epigone

Discipleship in the epigonic form is marked by distinctive traits and impulses. The original Epigoni were the sons of the seven heroes who led a successful war against Thebes, but, unlike their illustrious fathers, they failed to speak great words and accomplish famous deeds, proving unworthy of being immortalized in song and poetry and becoming nameless to future generations, being the "less distinguished successors of an illustrious generation."[1] For the epigone, there is little or nothing new to add to what was already said or done by persons greater than himself, and he feels awestruck by the master's ideas, believing these contain some powerful, irrefutable truths, "that economic system which the epigones in political economy contemplate with awe." If "the owl of Minerva spreads her wings at dusk"—to use Hegel's phrase—and if the epigone is one "born afterwards,"[2] then that spirit is not positioned to create anything new, being fated to bask in the twilight of the master's wisdom.

The epigone, then, is an undistinguished, partisan disciple who lacks creative vision and has a pronounced talent for turning the vital ideas of masters into rather mundane ones through unimaginative repetition. He finds an intellectual center by strongly identifying with his master's ideas and person, and often has a superficial grasp of his complex analyses and animating passions. Without true intellectual self-sufficiency and emotional independence, the epigone refuses to question seriously the veracity of the master's theoretical and methodological assumptions, and is eager to show loyalty by criticizing his teacher's rivals and detractors. Because the epigone neither generates new value-perspectives nor adds exciting intellectual elements to a theory, he is content to explain "what the master really meant," and his scholarship consists either of sympathetic explication of the master's ideas or work that reflects the teacher's paradigms.

Clearly, hero-worship marks the epigone; he believes the master has qualities that place him high above ordinary intellectuals, including noble traits of character, a powerful sense of mission, passionate vision, and striking intellect. The master's charisma acts as a strong magnet to attract and hold disciples, especially the young and unformed who feel gratitude to him for illuminating a bewildering world of tragedies, paradoxes and ambiguities, and for unlocking the secrets of perfecting public life. Masters who project intellectual certainty and strength of character naturally appeal to anxious and tentative spirits, and epigonic discipleship is inviting to those who seek a center by identifying with another.

The epigonic disciple, particularly if he formed close personal bonds with a living master, sometimes introjects into his own outlook some of the teacher's prejudices, whether loves, hatreds, hopes and fears, and may not be above imitating some of his personal mannerisms and life-style. Since the epigone has received a theoretical education that is identity-forming, guilt may be experienced if he fails to engage dutifully in missionary activity on behalf of the master's theories or fails to defend him against detractors. Blind adulation can prevent the epigonic disciple admitting, or even seeing, the master's defects, preferring to idealize the teacher as having unified thought and action to live an exemplary life while sometimes suffering from a neglectful or hostile world. The danger is that the epigone becomes a caricature of the teacher, orbiting as a planet around a powerful radiant sun to receive illumination and warmth, capable only of reflecting light and never generating it.

Following a master's death, the closest disciples often feel an impulse to elaborate the teacher's methods and to distill the rich oral teachings and writings into lucid axioms of meaning. The epigonic activity of

clarifying and summarizing may result in the master's
theories becoming darkened, either from a paucity of
insight or from distortions, for subtle ideas are easily
perverted by zealous or inept disciples when the master is unable to explain the proper weights of theoretical elements, to clarify ambiguities, and to settle interpretive disputes.

The passing of the master poses another problem.
If disciples fail to achieve some basic consensus about
the essential identity and implications of the master's
teaching, and conceptual differences sharpen, then ri-
valries may break out among them to establish who
will have pride of place as the leading interpreter. When
issues remain unresolved, the disciples may fragment
into distinct, hostile groups that each claim to represent the true teaching and rightful line of succession;
but if one group achieves hegemony over the others,
its versions of the master's teaching become established
as orthodox traditions that serve as standards to fix
the boundary between the acceptable and heretical.

Over time it becomes more difficult to be certain
whether the deceased master's teachings are being perceived in their original significance or through the impure accretions introduced by epigones. A further
complication ensues. The disciples who personally
knew the master teach the doctrine to persons who
never studied with the great teacher; and disciples who
"disciple" can impose on others their moral and in-

tellectual prejudices, passing these off to the unaware as presumed insights of their master. The "discipling disciples" claim that by virtue of knowing and loving the master, and sometimes because they were given special responsibilities, they are uniquely positioned to understand and teach the true doctrine.

Bernstein

The creative revisionist claims loyalty to his master's theories, while actually extending their conceptual meanings and practical applications. Revisions of theories often occur in periods of rapid historical change when novel patterns appear in the fabric of society and crisis challenges the explanatory powers of theories and forces attention on their problems and ambiguities. Creative revisionists, then, are disciples who alter their masters' theories to save these from petrification or extinction, and innovations are always accompanied by extensive quotations from the masters' texts, a useful technique to justify revisions as inherently "reasonable." Theoretical revision is naturally controversial because orthodox interpretations are challenged. Let us briefly examine the ideas of Eduard Bernstein to exemplify some general patterns that characterize the disciple as creative revisionist.

Bernstein published *Evolutionary Socialism* when

Marxist ideas experienced a fundamental intellectual crisis sparked by unforeseen novelties in capitalist economic and political development. To educate people to "recognize the inconsistency of tradition with what exists,"[3] and to revise Marx in light of new circumstances, were Bernstein's aims. His pointing to "gaps and contradictions" in Marx's theories was necessary and constructive; after all, "the further development of the Marxist doctrine must begin with a criticism of it."[4]

And surely Marx and Engels "left to their successors the duty of bringing unity again into their theory and of coordinating theory and practice."[5] Bernstein attacked Marx's "orthodox" followers for "everlastingly repeating the words of their masters" in dogmatic fashion, and for failing to confront basic theoretical issues at a time when Marxist teaching was threatened."[6] Instead, the orthodox waited patiently for the "inevitable" proletarian revolution that Marx predicted, unwilling to see that capitalism had softened its harmful impact.

The dramatic improvement of the workers' political and economic conditions cast severe doubt on the scientific validity of Marx's prediction of class warfare. Bernstein pointed to the growth of trade unions and legal social-democratic parties in raising the workers' living standard, in shortening the work-day, in securing their civil rights, and in expanding their political power. Marx's picture of society composed of two unified, opposed classes seemed outdated because of the increasing differentiation of roles and statuses: "the modern wage earners are not of the homogenous mass, devoid in an equal degree of property... as the *Communist Manifesto* foresees"[7]; and the "enormous increase of social wealth is not accompanied by a decreasing number of large capitalists but by an increasing number of capitalists of all degrees."[8]

And Marx's theory of surplus value "as the measure of the actual exploitation of the worker by the capitalist" struck Bernstein as unable to account for the failure of the workers to develop the degree of revolutionary consciousness that their "objective" oppression required.[9]

Bernstein affirmed that Marx's descriptions of capitalist laws were valid only for that system's early developmental stages; but the master mistakenly thought that the real contradictions he found "would recur in the future in always sharper forms and in great acuteness."[10]

And Marx confused issues by sometimes envisioning the workers' liberation taking place by sheer will-power and moral outrage; at other times he belied himself by visualizing revolution as guaranteed by deterministic laws of development that transcended human will. The relative weights of material, necessitarian forces in moving history compared to those controlled by free subjects remain obscure. For Bernstein, the evolution of capitalism since Marx's death proved the decisive importance of non-economic factors in explaining material and political change: "modern society is much richer than earlier societies in ideologies which are not determined by economics," and "economic development today leaves the ideological, and especially the ethical... greater space for independent activity."[11]

The workers were admonished to spend their precious time organizing themselves into "a democratic, socialistic party of reform"[12] because new historical conditions placed real limits on both revolutionary imagination and concrete political action. For Bernstein, it is dangerous, unrealistic dogma to urge the workers to be heroic risk-takers and provoke useless violence against stereotypical evil capitalists; instead, it is more rational to avoid romanticizing the workers' power and vision: "We have to take working men as they are. And they are neither so universally pauperized as was set out [by Marx]... nor so free from prejudices and weakness as their courtiers [the orthodox] wish to make us believe."[13] The workers ought to reject revolutionaries who offer "preconceived theories about the drift of the [socialist] movement... without an ever vigilant eye upon facts and experiences," for these siren calls inevitably "pass into Utopianism."[14]

Bernstein's revisions naturally stirred great controversy; he was vociferously attacked by defenders of the orthodox faith such as Karl Kautsky who denounced his ideas as "an abandonment of the fundamental prin-

ciples and concepts of scientific socialism."[15] Bernstein
struck back, affirming that he, like Kautsky, "had sprung
from the Marx-Engels school,"[16] and told how Marx
and Engels "have exercised the greatest influence on
my socialist line of thought."[17] Not only were his revisions guided by the masters' spirits, but they are entirely justified by careful readings of their texts. How
could Kautsky and others claim Bernstein was a renegade if Engels "honored me with his personal friendship not only till his death but who showed beyond the
grave, in his testamentary arrangements, a proof of his
confidence in me."[18] The disciple had received the
master's blessing!

Was Bernstein the saviour of Marxism who made
it effectual and timely, giving it sensitivity to new conditions by renouncing rigid, dogmatic accretions imposed by uncreative epigones? Or did he radically distort or water-down Marx to deplete fatally his
originally powerful vision? Of course the issue of
Bernstein's status in the Marxist tradition hinges on
how the texts of Marx and Engels are interpreted as a
whole, and what specific elements of these are high-
lighted or darkened. Clearly, decisions about what
Marx really "meant" are not easily made, for great
theories are richly ambiguous, inviting vastly divergent interpretations by rival creative-revisionists (com-
pare Lenin with Bernstein) who justify their disparate
views by quotes from the same master-texts. My judg-

ment is that while Bernstein strained classical Marxism to its limits, he did not intend to found a new theory but to save an endangered one. However, it is sometimes difficult to perceive the line between innovations that remain faithful to the spirit of a great theory and those that must destroy it.

Lenin and Bernstein are creative revisionists within the Marxist tradition, and perhaps Allen Bloom and Walter Berns occupy a similar status with regard to the discourse of academic political theory of their master-light, Leo Strauss.

Marx's orthodox faithful claimed his predictions rested on laws of universal necessity; and to question these laws meant to abandon the master himself. Bernstein disagreed, claiming that Marx was correct in his "general theory" of the "evolution of modern society" "but his "special deductions" were in error. The master had failed to estimate correctly the time required for the transition of capitalism to socialism and he gave insufficient weight to the possibilities of non-violent struggle in aiding that transition. However, the relative absence of an "acute opposition of things and classes" in advanced capitalism should not imply "the abandonment of the conquest of power organized politically and economically."[19]

Of course Bernstein claimed Marx and Engels' texts justified his revisions, and he urged Marxists to avoid theoretical dogmatism—to stop rejecting political compromise and negotiation as harmful to socialism. The orthodox were challenged to prove that capitalism inevitably produces unmanageable economic crises that necessitate violent revolution to abolish an unyielding, exploiting class: "If the universal crisis is the inherent law of capitalist production, it must prove its reality now or in the near future. Otherwise the proof of its inevitableness hovers in the air of abstract speculation."[20]

Nietzsche

A survey of Nietzsche's relationships to Schopenhauer and Wagner will help illuminate the nature of the dynamics involved in the rare journey of the spirit from discipleship to mastery.*

Nietzsche's Basel years found the young professor of Classical Philology thoroughly infatuated with Schopenhauer and Wagner, the two masters from whom he received theoretical educations. Schopenhauer of all thinkers "is the truest... ours is the age of Schopenhauer: a sane pessimism founded on the ideal, the seriousness of manly strength, the taste for what is simple and sane."[21]

Nietzsche's attraction to Wagner was due to their shared admiration for Schopenhauer and because he saw the Maestro as the living embodiment of the philosopher's ideal man: "I have found who reveals,

* An earlier version of this section on Nietzsche was published by the Wagner Society of Northern California.

as no other does, the image of what Schopenhauer calls the 'genius' [das Genie] and is penetrated through and through by that wonderfully deep philosophy [wundersam innigen Philosophie]."[22]

Wagner became Nietzsche's "mystagogue in the secret doctrines [in den Geheimlehren] of art and life,"[23] and the disciple remarked to his master:" I know of only one other man, your great spiritual brother [groben Geistes-brüder], Arthur Schopenhauer, whom I regard with equal reverence [Verehrung], even *religione Quadam*."[24]

Nietzsche's hero-worship was boundless and blind; he saw in them resonances of ancient Hellenic traits of intellect and spirit that made them superior to the greatest of the modern Germans, whether Goethe, Schiller or Holderlin: "there are between... Schopenhauer and Empedocles, Aeschylus and Richard Wagner such approximations and affinities [solche Nahen und Verwandtschaften] that one is reminded... of the very relative nature of all concepts of time [aller Zeitbegriffe]."[25]

This powerful adulation provided a perfect medium for the imprinting on him of his masters' intellectual paradigms, moral impulses and visions of a reborn German culture. Nietzsche, then, had been fully "discipled" by Schopenhauer and Wagner. He wrote numerous letters to friends proclaiming their exemplary virtues, dedicated several books to them, including the Birth of Tragedy (1872), Schopenhauer as Educator (1874) and Wagner at Bayreuth (1876); and their theories and cultural ideals shaped his intellectual horizons and language of analysis. Of what did Nietzsche's theoretical educations from his masters consist?

Schopenhauer viewed himself as a philosophical pessimist and "untimely man" who rejected the optimistic spirit of a scientific age that promised, through increasing enlightenment, to banish ignorance and material suffering and to perfect the social and human qualities. Also, he sharply criticized Hegel's teaching that history is progressive, moved by a tormented cosmic Spirit that transforms the whole of reality in its odyssey toward more rational forms of self-comprehension. For Schopenhauer, scientific rationalism and Hegel's historicism offered humanity false hopes, and could provide no true values on which to found a healthy, vital culture.

At the center of Schopenhauer's philosophy is his concept of the Will [Wille], the cosmic force that gives rise to all existents, from the inanimate, whether stones, water, air and fire, to living things, whether single-celled amoebas, plants, zebras or humans. The Will, then, is the *noumena* that differentiates itself into an abundance of forms and becomes visible as *phenomena*. Further, living beings are driven by a blind urge for survival, and are naturally marked by endless conflict, unfulfilled desires, misery and sudden death.

Schopenhauer rejected the traditional idea of a God of reason and justice who redeems the worthy from suffering according to a rational plan of salvation. Instead, the cosmic Will is neither good nor evil; it simply is, being oblivious to its own nature, and human beings have no intrinsic purposes to fulfill. Man is one with nature, partaking of her sublimity and horror, and he comes into being only to pass away again, suffering the curse of individuation in the time between birth and death.

This darkness is broken by a ray of hope. From torment and anxiety over senseless death may arise an impulse toward metaphysical sensitivity in a few spirits. They inquire into the identity of the cosmic Will, the meaning of suffering, and the value of existence. Schopenhauer claimed that metaphysics is the preserve of genius, most fully actualized in the philosopher, artist and saint. These rare persons heroically master their desires, anxieties and drive for mere survival to liberate their consciousness to serve as a mirror of the cosmic Will—a "world-eye" that both illuminates and communicates to others the eternal archetypes of the singular force in its infinite play of appearances. Schopenhauer judged that music, plastic art and tragic-drama are powerful mediums for expressing insight into the Will's many-sided identity. Metaphysical wisdom teaches that the pursuit of wealth, power and status are ephemeral and sources of suffering, and that conflict can neither be abolished nor the human estate perfected. However, it is possible to find momentary solace and relief from the burdens of life through metaphysical insight that lifts people from their egoistic concerns and private suffering to see they are one, participating in a common species-life of recurring situations, emotions, conflicts and dreams. For Schopenhauer, the ultimate affirmation of wisdom is for the self to engage in a Buddhistic negation of his *principium individuationis* to end suffering and to experience nirvanic unity with the primordial Will.

Nietzsche for a time perceived Wagner as the genius who actualized Schopenhauer's world-view into the realm of culture. His great operas seemed to unite metaphysics, tragic-drama and music into an organic whole to portray the universal traits of existence. Further, Wagner saw himself as a profound theoretician privileged with rare insight into the essence of ancient Greek culture, claiming to have found in that bygone world, particularly in Athens, an enviable harmony of reason and passion, of individuality and community, and of the city with the cosmic order. The Greeks impressed him as having created a vital Schopenhauerian "metaphysical culture" in which tragic-drama gave suffering archetypal meaning. They lived a life of shared concerns to overcome individual isolation, taking seriously the responsibilities of citizenship, attending theatre and practicing religious rituals together, and having a common reservoir of music, epic-poetry and myth that enabled them to communicate powerful feelings and experiences.

Wagner conducted his life as a holy mission to revitalize the German spirit, finding it barbaric and decadent, and lacking in a noble, public culture. Everywhere he found the reign of optimistic rationalism, and claimed this spirit was thoroughly superficial and downright destructive, for, when its utopian promises of progress failed, people would experience catastrophic despair, lacking solid ground on which to stand. Wagner criticized German educational institutions for malforming the young by teaching them hedonistic, materialist values, for failing to give creative expression to their myriad passions, and for socializing them into Hegel's philosophy instead of pointing them toward Schopenhauer, that lonely and neglected voice crying in the wilderness. And he judged that faulty education had corrupted the German language, filling it with "foreign" accretions that prevented rich contact with the wisdom and feelings embodied in the epic poetry and myth of the Volk. Wagner, then, saw himself as a modern Aeschylus whose Bayreuth movement, through repeated performances of his *gesamtkunstwerke*, would renew the German spirit by giving birth to a tragic culture.

Nietzsche's avid identification with the ideals and

theories of Schopenhauer and Wagner led him, for much of the Basel period, to be their defender and advocate, and his own writings show the indelible stamps of their intellectual worlds. Profoundly influenced by their spirits, he placed himself on a collision course with his profession and wrote powerful cultural criticism. He accused classical scholars of failing to understand the pessimistic base of Greek culture and how tragic-drama contained metaphysical wisdom that brought joyful relief to suffering. And he criticized German educational institutions for inculcating in the young wrong-headed values, for not providing the necessary conditions for the cultivation of genius; and he castigated leading intellectuals for supporting the false teachings of scientific rationalism and Hegelian historicism. Nietzsche defended in word and deed Wagner's Bayreuth movement of cultural renewal, and his association with the Maestro and Schopenhauer's pessimistic philosophy made him less a dispassionate scholar to many than an emotional apologist for his controversial masters. These constant tensions led Nietzsche to conclude that a University career was increasingly incompatible with pursuing the philosophical life and working for cultural renewal.

Remaining an epigone was not to be Nietzsche's destiny, for stirring within his spirit were doubts about the intellectual paradigms and cultural ideals that he

learned. Even while Nietzsche was publicly lauding
Wagner, he began to voice serious criticisms of him in
his private notes, accusing him of being vain and am-
bitious, overbearing in his personal relations, an actor
who enjoyed theatrical effects for their own sake, and
he wondered whether his master's music-dramas really had affinities to the Hellenic spirit. This disinte-
gration of Nietzsche's emotional and intellectual ties
to Wagner quickened at the first Bayreuth festival, the
moment when performing the Ring cycle would signal the birth of a new and healthy German culture.
Nietzsche could not bear what he saw at Bayreuth; he
concluded that Wagner's art catered to the worst elements in German society, that his music was overly
romantic, filled with oceanic feelings and bombastic
sounds, and that he, Nietzsche, had been unhappily
seduced by Wagner's vision. The breaking of bonds to
Wagner was accompanied by severe criticism of
Schopenhauer as well, for his former masters were in-
separably linked in his mind's eye.

Leaving discipleship behind was not easy; to the
contrary, the end of the Basel period found Nietzsche
experiencing severe physical and emotional problems,
barely able to carry out his academic duties, and feeling exceedingly uncertain about his future. He later
judged this difficult time as symptomatic of his growing recognition that his "deeper self" [jenes unterste
Selbst][26] had "been buried and grown silent under

the continual pressure of having to listen to other selves [unter einembestandigen Horen-Mussen auf andre Selbste]," and further, "thanks to it alone [his illness], I was torn away from an estimate of my life task [Lebens-Aufgabe] which was not only false but a hundred times too low [zu niedrigen Auffassung]."[27] The days of discipleship marked the time when Nietzsche sought "repose in a trusted friendship... with no suspicion or question marks [ohne Verdacht and Fragezeichen]...,"[28] but with the unfortunate consequence of having "willfully closed my eyes to Schopenhauer's blind will to morality [blindem Willen zur Moral]... I had deceived myself about Richard Wagner's incurable romanticism [unheilbare Romantik]... about the Greeks; similarly about the Germans and their future."[29] Illness, then, enabled Nietzsche to recognize what his emotional attachments retarded seeing, namely, that discipleship to others was incompatible with achieving his independent path of theorizing.

Nietzsche was acutely aware of the spiritual stages he traversed in his journey from discipleship to mastery; and he thought his experiences contained universal lessons: "As it happened to me... so must it happen to everyone in whom a task wants to take form [in dem eine Auf-gabe leibhaft werden] and 'come into the world.'"[30] The first "decisive event" [sein entscheidendes Ereigniss] for a disciple destined to become a "free-spirit" [der Typus freier Geist] is the "great separation [grosse Loslosung],"[31] and this is only possible if one was previously a "bound spirit [gebundener Geist]... chained forever to his corner, to his post."[32] Discipleship entails having no true intellectual or moral identity apart from the master, and leads to being imprisoned by powerful ties of loyalty and affection, by "that awe [jene Ehrfurcht] which befits the young, their diffidence and delicacy before all that is time-honored and dignified... gratitude for the ground out of which they grew, for the hand that led them, for the shrine where they learned to worship [fur das Heiligthum, wo sie anbeten lernten]...."[33]

The disciple who would exorcise the master from himself is inevitably committing a partial act of self-destruction; for cutting away the master means removing those parts of himself that needed another to gain substance. The recognition of having been blindly dependent precipitates a spiritual experience akin to a great "earthquake" [wie ein Erdstoss] in which the "soul is devastated, torn loose, torn out...."[34] The former master becomes a negative identity, an unworthy ground of being, and the unfettered spirit says to itself: "'Better to die than live here'[Lieber sterben als hier leben]... and this 'here,' this 'at home' is everything which it had loved until then."[35] But the tormented spirit cannot return to its former identity or make whole what it has broken apart; it can only feel a "sudden horror and suspicion [ein plotzlicher Schrecken undArgwohn] of that which it loved...."[36] The master, then, has been scaled-down to "human, all too human" size; he is perceived as a flawed human being without special wisdom or exemplary moral greatness.

This "first outburst of strength and will to self-determination [von Kraft und Willen zur Selbstbestimmung], self-valorization, this will to free will [zum freien Willen]" while an essential stage in shedding discipleship, can become a terminal "disease" because the new found freedom may end in formless-ness.[37] Lacking firm ground on which to stand, having rejected the master and his traditions of theorizing, the free-spirit neither knows its own possibilities and lim-its nor can it affirm new ideas and values, having not found its way to a new conceptual paradigm. Further, it lacks calmness and maturity, is filled with anger, con-tempt, pride and unbridled curiosity, and is unable to trust anyone to guide it, for fear it will become fettered once again.

In this turbulent spiritual condition, the former disciple "wanders about savagely with an unsatisfied lust [mit einer unbefriedigten Lustern-heit]... he rips apart what attracts him. With an evil laugh [bosen Lachen] he overturns what he finds concealed, spared until then by some shame."[38] Delight is found in un-veiling as seedy what most people revere; and he "creeps curiously and enticingly around what is most forbidden [um das Verbotenste schleicht],"[39] wondering what secret pleasures they contain. Nothing is sacred to the experimental spirit who asks: "Cannot all values be overturned [alle Werthe umdrehn]? And is good perhaps evil [Bose]? And God only an invention [Erfindung], a nicety of the devil?"[40] The boundary between illusion and reality breaks apart for him; his thoughts travel to distant places few have visited or even conceived; and the result is that" Loneliness [Einsamkeit] surrounds him, curls around him, even more threatening, strangling, heart-constricting [Herzzuschnurender]...."[41]

If the spirit is not defeated or destroyed by its "morbid isolation [krankhaften Vereinsamumg], from the desert of these experimental years [Versuchs-Jahre]"— the time when it tested his own powers and boundaries, explored new theories and moral values, and sifted and weighed the masters who formed it—then it may overcome its nihilistic rage and self-defeating curiosity and move to a new stage: "that mature freedom of the spirit which is fully as much self-mastery and discipline of the heart [Zucht des Herzens], and which permits paths to many opposing ways of thought."[42]

The former disciple, then, has found his way to himself; he gives form to his rich impulses for knowledge, and because he achieved the "great health [der grossen Gesundheit]," it is possible to generate thoughts from an experience of overfullness. Further, resentment against the former masters has ceased; they are no longer controlling presences, but persons who take their proper place as part of his history of becoming who he is. In this condition the theoretical mind is free to soar, "No longer chained down by hatred and love [nicht mehr in den Fesseln vonLiebe und Hass], one lives withoutYes and No, voluntarily near, voluntarily far... now the free spirit concerns himself only with things—and how many there are!—which no longer trouble him [welche ihn nicht mehrbekummern]."[43]

Nietzsche now strove to develop new interpretive paradigms to diagnose and cure the cultural illnesses he found in modern life, tracing the nihilistic spiritual crisis of theWest to the values of Socrates and Christ, the figures who gave impulse to forms of thinking and moralizing that formed a genealogical heritage, shaping the course of European cultural development and making possible the rise of modern science with its optimistic expectation of endless progress through mastery of nature's laws. Nietzsche judged that traditional values were in decline and crisis because accepting these had led people to experience life as vacuous and filled with untenable contradictions.

Christianity taught that bodily desires, the natural beauty of the physical world and self-love are sources of evil temptation that endanger the soul and prevent its passage to a perfect, transcendent spiritual place, thereby slandering for Nietzsche the intrinsic beauty, dignity and worthiness of earthly life. And its teaching that selflessness, pity and unconditional love are the highest qualities of the good human being, led people to become hypocrites, attempting to practice unrealizable moral precepts that conflicted with the requirements of living, inevitably resulting in unwarranted guilt and self-hatred. Philosophy, too, participated in abnegating life because it elevated a truncated concept of reason to the highest rank, radically separating it from the "impure" passions and intuitions that threatened its capacity for objective, impersonal contemplation. Nietzsche criticized the "ascetic ideal" as productive of nihilism, whether in morals, philosophy or science, denied that reason can fathom timeless being and eliminate the transience of time with its play of appearances, or provide unconditional moral standards to guide conduct in subtle and changing human situations.

Nietzsche's thinking did not rest content with unmasking the seediness of traditional idols and values; he theorized about the need for new concepts and ideals to transfigure Western culture and give joy to the depleted and nihilistic human spirit. He taught that the essence of life is expressed in the will-to-power, that is, the drive that gives form and harmony to the multiple demands that characterize life and that threaten to tear it apart. Further, the higher human type (Übermensch) welcomes richness of experience, delights in perspective and appearance, and integrates reason and passion to become a complete person. And he is characterized by Dionysian pessimism, an attitude toward life that affirms its worth and joy even in the midst of experiencing contradiction and suffering. He preached the doctrine of eternal recurrence as a new metaphysical religion to imbue momentary experiences with the aspect of eternity, thereby abolishing the destructive, dualistic forms of thought he claimed to find in the older metaphysical and religious traditions.

Nietzsche transfigured rather than abolished the theoretical educations he received from Schopenhauer and Wagner, and his thought maintains family resemblances to their conceptual paradigms and moral impulses. A brief discussion of Nietzsche's post-disciple relationship to Schopenhauer offers some insight into the processes by which new theories grow from older ones, and how the new expresses both identity and difference with the respect to the old.

Nietzsche's theorizing is clearly prophetic, oriented toward crisis, and concerned with diagnosing how hegemonic values shape culture and politics to either enhance or diminish the experience of communal life. These concerns also mark Schopenhauer who taught that German culture is a "wasteland"; and while Nietzsche disagrees with him about the causes of cul-

tural illness and the nature of the appropriate cura-
tive values, he shares with him some common ways of
theorizing, both stylistic and substantive, assuredly
learned in his phase of discipleship.

For example, Nietzsche consciously posited the
will-to-power as the alternative to Schopenhauer's will-
to-live; and his drive to correct Schopenhauer about
the nature of the "will" indicates a process by which
new theoretical elements grew from conflict with older
ones. Nietzsche's claim that affirming life in the face
of suffering is more noble than abolishing pain through
a nirvanic negation of the ego shows, once again, that
Schopenhauer established the theoretical field of concerns that the former disciple addressed, negated and
finally transfigured. Also, Nietzsche's rejection of pity
and selflessness as virtues, and his criticism of Christian morality as grounded in the spirit of resentment,
can be partly understood as reactions to his education by Schopenhauer, for his teacher had made pity
and selfless love cornerstones of his ethical philosophy, and the former disciple felt compelled to rectify
his errors.

Nietzsche wondered how life can be lived to experience eternity, the plenitude of being, in the transient, ever-altering moment, thereby feeling transcendence in what is immanent. This drive to find eternity
in the oscillations of mood, perspective and in the perpetual flux of time, also mark Schopenhauer's out-

look, having taught that subjects at rare moments of self-loss can perceive the imperishable archetypes of things in ordinary, finite experiences, thereby overcoming the duality of the Will as *noumena* and *phenomena*. And while Nietzsche rejected his educator's theory that the experience of timelessness requires the negation of the *principium individuationis*, he nonetheless is theorizing along lines he learned from Schopenhauer, believing with his teacher that the reconciliation of being and time is a noble endeavor.

Characteristic of Nietzsche is his concern with the spiritual qualities of the "higher man" who can overcome nihilism and affirm life as a joyful abundance of richnesses. This theorizing about the nature of the great human being grew from the rich soil of Schopenhauer's thinking about the identity and vocation of the "genius." And there is little doubt that Nietzsche's enduring interest in fathoming the significance of music, tragedy and metaphysics for the quality of human life—along with his critiques of scientific rationalism and historicism—reflect the lasting importance of the theoretical education Schopenhauer gave him. However, how Nietzsche began as a Schopenhauerian [and Wagnerian] and became an original master clearly deserves much fuller treatment.

CHAPTER SIX

Masters, Disciples and the University

Academic Epigones

Most of us have implicit or explicit views of what teaching in the University is and ought to be, concepts about the nature of its traditions, and judgments and feelings about the division of academic fields into schools with divergent, sometimes conflicting values, assumptions, and methods. As teachers and scholars, we often affirm our devotion to finding truth through questioning and discussion, and as educators in my own field of political theory, we aim at improving public life by diagnosing its maladies and by proposing principles of justice and community well-being. Indeed, we think that political theory is, or at least ought to be, a noble vocation composed of moral ideals and intellectual aspirations which should remain free of partisan concerns that distort vision and narrow judgment.

My general claim is that discipleship may favor the growth of an epigonic spirit that imperils the deeper impulses of intellectual life, threatening to turn it into an impoverished activity conducted by like-minded persons who have difficulty discoursing across parochial groups that encourage intellectual conformity and the loss of critical capacity. Disciples who cluster in schools are not only prone to develop esoteric languages and special concepts that favor rigid ideology, but they propogate their favorite ideas and methods across generational lines, using academic institutions as power bases to advance their special causes and to recruit new followers; and they often praise, without the slightest hint of disagreement, the views and persons of their masters while sometimes actually deforming their ideas and values. As educators we have the obligation of helping students develop critical, evaluative abilities essential to independent thinking and judging; and while we generally claim to do these things, I fear that the opposite often occurs, with a consequent degradation of teachers, students, and educational values.

The following remarks about the institutionalization of discipleship in the university rests on a guiding assumption: namely, that there is a growing epigonic spirit among faculty who often use their positions to proselytize special views and vie with one another to capture the hearts and minds of students.

We have in the Academy an unhappy situation wherein some first-generation epigonic disciples teach their masters' traditions of discourse to students whose education leads some of them to become second-generation epigones. The real danger is that education becomes institutionalized and tame, the preserve of a dominant epigonic spirit lacking the ability to inspire new generations of students to become thoughtfully perplexed and independent, the essential conditions from which can emerge a vital life of the mind.

The fragmentation of the disciples into distinct, hostile groups claiming to represent the true teaching and rightful line of succession may, if the issues between them remain unresolved, result in permanent splits and continuous emnity. However, if one faction achieves hegemony over the others, its versions of the master's teaching become established as "orthodox" traditions that fix the boundary between the acceptable and heretical. Naturally as time passes it is more difficult to decide whether the deceased master's doctrines are perceived in their original significance or through the impure accretions introduced by epigoni. A further complication ensues when epigoni who personally knew the master transmit doctrine to a new generation of learners. Disciples who "disciple" may impose on others their own moral and intellectual prejudices, passing these off as privileged statements of the master's teaching, as if their personal contact with the master ensures they know the truth of his doctrine.

I do not wish to give the false impression that every variety of discipleship must be dismissed as uniformly undesirable. Indeed, there may exist a healthy form of discipleship that is distinguishable from its pathological, epigonic variety. A healthy form of discipleship is incompatible with blind partisanship, hero worship of the master, and the loss of critical ability. Part of what disciples do is to keep alive traditions by commenting upon, and enriching, the ideas, values, methods embodied in these. Without the transmission of master-academic perspectives on the nature of political theory, and on the great texts that comprise it, the young would lose something irreplaceably valuable from their experience, namely, ways of thinking deeply and systematically about the nature of civic life, with its issues of justice, power, equality, virtue, freedom, and institutional patterns. If the young are never taught what must be remembered, then a silent void comes to be, signifying that irreplaceable parts of human cultural experience no longer exist to be reflected upon; and without such reflection, we cannot morally improve, become wiser, or live creatively within the paradoxes and ambiguities of existence.

Master-Academics

Today there are no master-thinkers whom we know of inside or outside the University of the rank of a Socrates, Plato, Aristotle, Rousseau, Hegel, Marx,

Hobbes, Tocqueville, Nietzsche, or Weber. It follows that the many contemporary teachers and scholars of political theory learned their subject matter in graduate school directly from famous master-academics or, more frequently, from their disciples.

Since truly influential master-academics who found schools are few in number, it is disciples who propagate their doctrines by communicating these orally to students, by writing books and articles to explain and apply their concepts, and by founding journals as forums to publish largely sympathetic material. Disciples often network together to help the most promising students find academic posts to help ensure that the teachings of their favorite master-academics remain alive by being transmitted to new generations of students. Clearly, many graduate students today learn political theory from the perspectives of disciples who feel impelled, with varying degrees of intensity, to further one-sided, partisan views. Just as Plato's poets and painters in the *Republic* portray in words and pictures "appearances of appearances," remaining oblivious to the joy of bathing their minds directly in the luminous Ideas, so it seems that many political theory students learn their subject secondhand from epigonic disciples who fail to communicate deeply and powerfully the original experiences, passions, problems and dilemmas that preoccupied the few master-thinkers and the more numerous master-academics.

Why do some master-academics found schools and attract disciples whereas others do not? Allow me a few remarks using Hannah Arendt to exemplify the issues. My speculations are that she neither founded, nor wished to, a school of political theory, that her thinking lacks qualities attractive to potential disciples, and that she deliberately avoided engaging in what I earlier called theoretical education, although she certainly continues to exert great influence on contemporary scholarship. Arendt's theorizing strikes me as not readily translatable into clear-cut maxims, propositions and concepts that together comprise an orderly, easily understood ideational world, perhaps the consequence of her refusal to claim to possess an authoritative method for interpreting great texts, and because she makes no serious attempt to treat the history of political theory as a unified tradition of discourse with defining impulses and clear overall goals. Her absence of a "system" challenges readers perpetually to fathom her meaning; she evokes perplexity; and her thought has a tragic, pessimistic character that fails to lead potential disciples to think she offers clear-cut solutions to the problems of public life posed by modernity. Arendt refuses to reduce the rich complexities of historical and political experience to simplistic choices between unambiguous forms of good and evil. Young theorists who drink from her well, therefore, do not become disciples who project airs of certainty.

"Discipling disciples" who follow different master-academics are prone to intertribal conflicts, accusing one another of committing serious moral and intellectual errors, such as neither appreciating their favorite masters' personal character, nor their teachings about the traditions, history and methods of political theory. Sometimes competition breaks out among "discipling disciples" from different schools to capture the minds and hearts of potential followers, and the overly-enthusiastic in both religion and political theory may find it difficult to tolerate or understand, ideas that seem dissonant to values and beliefs that partly regulate their intellectual and emotional experiences, often preferring to forgo serious communication with persons who are not members of their circle.

If conflicts sometimes occur between members of different academic schools of political theory, then conflicts also are found among disciples of the same school, usually but not exclusively when their master dies. The death of the master leaves a void. Strong disagreements appear among followers over the true identity of the master's ideas and values, over whether his doctrine should be modified in light of changing circumstances, and the most influential disciples argue among themselves over which of them should legitimately assume his mantle of authority to settle doctrinal disputes and assume leadership on issues pertaining to the school's welfare.

Much as Socrates ironically affirmed his ignorance, claiming he knew only that he knew nothing, being a simple searcher for truth, so Strauss, Voegelin and Wolin as master-academics would likely deny they consciously sought disciples to propagate their teachings. Still, it is not unjust to speculate that the three were motivated to attract followers for reasons not unlike those that mark some of the seminal political theorists, including: to seek personal validation by expressions of adulation and affection; to have their ideas sympathetically clarified and disseminated; to shape practice in the public world by educating the influential to their teachings; and to circumvent the oblivion of anonymity by having their persons and teachings live in the memory of others.

What general qualities do Strauss, Voegelin and Wolin share? They wrote first-rank works that treat the history of political theory as a tradition of discourse marked by distinct traits and impulses, and each gave thoughtful and powerful interpretations of political theory's canonical writers. Further: they offer pictures of the modern age as crisis ridden and undermining of older insights of political thought and practice; they saw themselves as having missions to set the public world on healthy foundations by healing the illnesses they diagnosed in the body-politic; they attracted excellent students because of their personal charisma, intellectual accomplishments, and claims to have special vision; they have followers whose writings show the imprints of their theories and who proselytize on their behalf; and they have, or had, control of journals wherein disciples explain and disseminate their points of view, along with having professional panels, and formal or informal associations, devoted to them.

Briefly stated, what basic concepts did Strauss, Voegelin and Wolin teach their students that became institutionalized as normal discourse in academic political theory?

Strauss's disciples learn there are "transhistorical truths" and "three waves of modernity," that Machiavelli is a "teacher of evil," that one of the great intellectual conflicts of our time is that between "ancients and moderns," with the nihilism-prone moderns often displaying propensities to "tyranny," "historicism," "moral relativism," and narrow-minded "scientific positivism." Not only has "political philosophy declined," but also the classical views of Aristotle contain the "true science of politics" and ought to be resurrected. Followers of Strauss's teaching learn distinctions between "natural right" and "natural law," between "ancient and modern liberalism," between "exoteric and esoteric" readings of great texts, and between "faith" and "reason" as exemplified in the classic conflict of Athens with Jerusalem.

Voegelin's disciples also share a distinctive linguistic world that sets them apart, and persons who fail to appreciate history, texts, and the "contemporary crisis" through their master's grids of meaning, often find they are treated as intellectual outsiders. His disciples use such terms as "cosmion," "symbols of order," "divine ground of existence," "gnosticism," "leap in being," "immanentization of the absolute," "ecumenicity," "universality," and "transcendence." Voegelin offers a "history of order" that probes into the various "symbolizations" available to consciousness, and through a "retheorization" and "therapeutic analysis" of history, it becomes possible to battle Gnostic heresies and to contact the largely forgotten "soteriological truths of Christian revelation."

Members of Wolin's school also have a common set of concepts. Political theory is conceived as a "special tradition of discourse" marked by a "continuity of preoccupations," and that theories are attempts at political education in times of great "crisis" in the fabric of public life of historical communities. Seminal theoretical works embody the "continuing dialogue of Western political speculation," and theorists make knowledge-claims directed to the "sphere of public judgments." Further, Wolin's followers emphasize certain motifs and ideas that set them apart from disciples of other master-academics, including the "need for community," "the primacy of politics," "civic virtue," "friendship," "epic and normal theory," the "decline of the political," "methodism," "decentralization," and the "vocation of the theorist."

Leaving aside the issue of the truth-value and overall merits of the ideas of Strauss, Voegelin and Wolin, my claim is that numbers of graduate students were "discipled" by learning from them rich languages filled with subtle conceptual distinctions, implicit rules for observing, describing and understanding politics, and ways of reading great texts. Students acquired teachings about political theory's basic impulses and insights; ideas about the inherent limits and possibilities of political life; views of what things and persons are worthy of love and hate; and judgments about what moral values and types of political activity are of higher and lower rank. Learned are ways of formulating questions and defining problems, basic ideas about the confines and possibilities of historical processes, metaphysical assumptions about the cosmic order, and views about the limits and potentials of human nature. Students come to discern what things and persons are worthy of reverence or fear, and further, they are taught what particular attitudes and conducts indicate allegiance to, and participation in, their masters' conceptual worlds.

The three claimed to have missions to save the community from its deleterious values, erroneous life-practices, and faulty political institutions; and they communicate, to their disciples, whether personally or through texts, strong ethical judgments.

Whether willfully or not, Strauss, Voegelin and Wolin offered some of their students inclusive and powerful intellectual and emotional experiences that proved identity-forming and enduring in impact, the preconditions for having disciples. As followers of Strauss, Voegelin and Wolin attained academic posts, they taught new generations of students their masters' ideas, and ensured institutional continuity and legitimacy for special forms of political-theoretical discourse.

To explore the general nature of the master/disciple relationship in the University and in the field of political theory, I will examine some of the traditional meanings of the terms "master" and "disciple" in the context of raising some central issues with respect to Strauss, Voegelin and Wolin as master-academics.

Master-academics are institutionally authorized to initiate activities students must follow—writing papers and theses, learning to speak clearly and thoughtfully in seminars, fulfilling requirements to receive course credit and advancement to candidacy for higher degrees—under threat of penalty for disobedience and poor performance. The masters decide which students will be granted doctorates, given moral support and letters of recommendation, aided in finding academic posts, and make crucial judgments about their students' personal character and qualities of intellect that impact on their futures. For their part, students not only depend on the good-will of the powerful for academic survival, but are sometimes overwhelmed by the reputations, titles, influence, and accomplishments of their famous teachers, experiences that supply the seeds from which an epigonic spirit may sprout.

It is unlikely that Strauss, Voegelin and Wolin either failed to appreciate the powers inherent in their academic positions and reputations, or their attractiveness to students wishing to learn their views. Some obvious questions follow: to what extent, and in what exact ways did the three use their influential posts, personal charisma and intellectual achievements to gain disciples by nurturing ideological conformity and by fostering strong personal bonds that may have retarded some of their students from achieving intellectual maturity and emotional independence? Further, if Strauss, Voegelin and Wolin saw themselves as engaging in ethical as well as mental formation, then what standards of value did they employ in their activities of educating?

Strauss, Voegelin and Wolin might well have generated authority in a manner analogous to excellent artisans who claim superior knowledge of the principles of their arts. To what extent, and in what specific respects, did Strauss, Voegelin and Wolin conceive of political theory as akin to an art governed by intrinsic rules, methods and concerns they expected students to learn? Further, what precise traits of intellect and moral character did they judge must be present for students to be worthy of personal instruction? Did they visualize the teacher/student relationship as partly analogous to the artisan/apprentice relationship, and did they make distinctions between esoteric and exoteric forms of teaching?

For example, Strauss partly attracted students (apprentices) by claiming to demonstrate special ways of interpreting canonical texts to uncover their original, largely buried meanings. He thought that such a hermeneutic art is governed by complex rules knowable by a wise master who communicates these directly to students he deems ready and worthy; and in turn, the students learn to see normally hidden meanings in theoretical texts. A climate conducive to discipleship might be fostered because empathetic imitation may lead students to absorb uncritically central features of the master's ways of seeing and treating textual materials—indeed, comprising a learning situation that may hold affinities to what occurs in the traditional artisan/apprentice relationship.

Clearly, Strauss, Voegelin and Wolin are not masters by virtue of being literally legal heads of households who dispose of living or inanimate property. Still, a few suggestive analogies can be drawn to invite discussion. Famous master-academics who attract disciples gain power, on varying levels, over their followers' intellectual and emotional lives; and further, this power is partly "legal" because it is rooted in, and legitimated by, the formal rules and customs that govern University teacher/student relationships, particularly at the level of graduate education. A master's superior power over dependent, weaker followers might, if we stretch things a bit, be seen as a non-traditional form of ownership; after all, charismatic masters shape the intellectual self-understandings of the young and impressionable.

What follows from this line of reasoning? For example, Plato's self-understanding as a philosopher with the mission to seek the Good was profoundly indebted to, hence partly "owned" by Socrates, his martyred and noble master who, even in death, continued to "possess" Plato sufficiently to lead him to write the great majority of his dialogues placing Socrates on center stage, portrayed in the fullness of life to posterity. Nietzsche's hero-worship of Schopenhauer and Wagner was so powerful during most of his years as a classical philologist at Basel that he proudly and unabashedly called himself their disciple, praised their virtues in books he dedicated to them, and alienated important classicists by serving as a leading apologist for their iconoclastic, controversial theories. The young Nietzsche's identity was partly "owned" by them.

Could similar forms of "possessing" and "owning" characterize the relationships of Strauss, Voegelin and Wolin with respect to some of their followers, particularly if the three truly founded academic schools of political theory, thereby making them, in effect, "heads of households" positioned to have lasting impacts on some of their students' intellects, moral and political values, and careers? It is of real interest to explore the ways, both hidden and obvious, that forms of "possessing" and "owning" took place among them, as well as examining the different attitudes they had about having followers.

Analogies between discipleship in political theory and in religion are inherently controversial, and I believe that Strauss, Voegelin and Wolin would likely reject suggestions that they share affinities to religious teachers, for they neither claim they are divinity become flesh nor that their ideas about the nature, history and tasks of political theory are grounded in, or justified by, revelation, preferring to defend their concepts through reasoned debate. Still, some analogies can be suggested to invite discussion. For example, the three might offer followers a type of "glad tidings"—the theoretical insights they claimed to possess about the sources of derangement in the public world, and wisdom about how to bring about improvements or cures in the body-politic, such as recapturing for our own age the ancient, classical understandings of the nature and ends of civic life, fighting against the evils of political gnosticism that have disrupted political existence, or creating small-scale communities to allow citizens to engage in political deliberation and action. Despite real and significant differences among them, the three would generally agree that political theory might heal and regenerate the public world; and that implies personal and spiritual renewal as well, since they think the political community's values, ways of life, and institutions entwine with the destiny of the *psyche*.

If, indeed, Strauss, Voegelin and Wolin saw themselves with missions to heal the public world, and if their closest followers believed them, seeing the three as charismatic models to emulate, then perhaps there surrounded them some "discipling disciples" who defended and spread their teachings. The "discipling" would occur among faculty, students, and the politically influential with the goal of educating them to their masters' points of view; and when possible, to build power bases in University administrations and Political Science departments to facilitate sympathetic faculty appointments, favorable committee composition, and suitable curricula. Further, the intellectual and moral conflicts that sometimes mark relations between empirical political scientists and political theorists, might be especially acute for students who studied with Strauss, Voegelin and Wolin because they learned that the "scientific" study of politics is an aberration, a fall from the wisdom of the Tradition, a destruction of the "classics," or an unholy modern Gnostic heresy. Some theory faculty are not above seeing themselves engaged in battle with evil forces that darken the perception of truth, justice and virtue. And the oblique message to the disciples is to vanquish and destroy the evil of empiricism—a crusade that some have carried out with great zeal.

It is not implausible to suggest that Strauss, Voegelin and Wolin might have developed axioms of belief and rules of behavior, whether implicit or explicit, to which disciples were expected to conform as a condition of being citizens of good-standing in their respective communities. This would imply that the violation of rules and standards carried a range of potential or actual "disciplines" which, depending on the exact nature of the infraction, might result in warnings, silent treatment, loss of friendships, rejection by the master, and banishment from the group. What general patterns and specific practices, then, characterize the ways the three "disciplined," and what are the key differences among them in these respects?

Errant disciples always pose problems for tightly-knit communities, and are often the target of harsh treatment. The "renegade" is the most dangerous because, as a former insider, he or she knows intimately the intellectual, moral and methodological ideas and practices of the school that is challenged. Further, the renegade often has deep insights into the master's personal strengths and weaknesses, and can use these to great advantage when attacking him. It is to be expected that Strauss, Voegelin and Wolin experienced at least a few followers leaving their fold to become errants and renegades. How did they individually perceive such events and how did they proceed to enforce discipline on former disciples who threatened the vitality and stability of their communities?

The Berkeley School: Wolin

Some biting remarks Wolin makes about Strauss in *Presence of the Past* shows that master-academics are not above promoting inter-school rivalry by teaching their disciples to harbor ill-feelings toward theories and persons judged competitors in wisdom.[1] Wolin portrays Strauss as a deceptive man whose calm surface exterior hid an interior of boundless vanity, an "erudite scholar whose retiring nature was in inverse proportion to his dreams of glory."[2] Of what did Strauss's drive for glory consist? Certainly not mere academic accomplishment and reputation! Instead, he is a shrewd founder of an "academic ideology" that attracts disciples and organizes them into "a compact, intensely loyal, doctrinally fastidious sect...,"[3] indeed, a religious-political movement that craves power in the state and the University.

To accomplish its goals, and to ensure its continuing survival and vitality, "Straussism" supports its followers "by fellowships and teaching positions...,"and "alerts the faithful to any changes in the doctrine."[4] Wolin smells "religious fundamentalism" because Strauss presumably taught his disciples to worship piously a "few written texts" he "believed to contain the truth.[5] Unfortunately, the discernment of the texts' "esoteric meanings" are open only to the "initiated" instructed in Strauss's special art of interpretation; and if the sect develops "internal differences," these are hidden to avoid breaking its "facade of unity to the outside world."[6] For Wolin, then, the cultish ethos of Straussism promotes a "Brüderschaft rather than a simple sodality," the former being a tightly-knit male dominated group with intense personal relations and a shared ethos; and further, the disciples revel in their rise from "apostolic poverty" to a powerful political and intellectual force as witnessed in the "apotheosis of its founder to a pedestal where he is beyond criticism."[7]

Although Wolin's comments may not be entirely unjust, they strike me as disingenuous and self-serving because of his history of resentment against Strauss and his followers that began nearly forty years ago with his, and Schaar's, vociferous attack on *Essays on the Scientific Study of Politics*, a collection of pieces edited by Herbert Storing with Strauss's sanction and personal direction. It is ironic and revealing that some of Wolin's negative remarks about Strauss and "Straussism" might also be leveled against himself and the "Berkeley school." For example, Wolin helped create an "academic ideology" that attracted disciples into a visible "sect" who share concepts of theorizing, modes of analyzing the "tradition," and populist, democratic values that provide the paradigms that guide much of their intellectual work. Certainly Wolin would not deny that he, as Strauss, also supported favorite students by helping them gain "fellowships and teaching positions," or that he too shared Strauss's "dreams of glory" with respect to achieving great influence in the University and the political community. The quest for power led Wolin [and Schaar] in the late 1960's at Berkeley to try unsuccessfully to leave the Political Science Department, with its "methodizing" anti-philosophical tendencies, to found a Department of Political Theory to teach students his own "esoteric" ideas about political theory, much as Strauss is accused of having done at Chicago. Wolin's creating the journal *Democracy* as a forum for him and his associates to express their political values, and to help reshape American politics in the desired directions by educating the well-placed and influential, certainly indicates drives for "glory" and power.

Wolin can hardly be said to worship in Strauss's manner "a few written texts" engraved with "esoteric meanings" that "contain the truth." Still, it not implausible that some of Wolin's readings of canonical writers, along with his interpretations of the traditions, vocation and contemporary plight of political theory, are as enigmatic and esoteric in several respects as those of Strauss. If Wolin cannot be accused of gathering his disciples into a Strauss-like "Brüderschaft," with its exclusive commitment to "masculine" moral and spiritual values, Wolin may have created a "sodality," an ecumenical, non-sexist form of intense fellowship that admits as members bright young men and women, but on condition that they equally and democratically conform to his Berkeley school's articles of faith. And if the Straussian movement has risen from "apostolic poverty" to a powerful educational and political force as witnessed in the "apotheosis of its founder to a pedestal where he is beyond all criticism," then is it just to fault Strauss for having the vision, shrewdness and doctrine in a combination that led to worldly success, or to admonish him because his disciples made of him an object of worship, something that Strauss might have resisted if he lived longer?

Peter Euben as Epigone

Peter Euben strikes me as Wolin's [and Schaar's] true epigone who, despite pronouncements to the contrary, is unable to overcome his emotional and intellectual subservience to his master(s).[8] He was a favorite student of theirs at UC Berkeley and later their colleague and close friend at UC Santa Cruz. In the preface to his recent *Tragedy of Political Theory*,[9] Euben not only offers some clues about the unique qualities of the Berkeley school, but illustrates some interesting and subtle traits of the epigonic spirit.

Wolin and Schaar are called "friends" by Euben, a concept particularly stressed by Schaar and often used by members of the "Berkeley school" to indicate they are "insiders" or initiates who have common concerns, a shared language of theorizing, and a sense of mutual obligation. [Schaar's grounding of his intellectual work in his circle of friends is briefly alluded to on p. vii of his *Legitimacy and the Modern State*[10]]. Euben describes Schaar as a "treasured colleague who has reminded me of my insufficiencies in moments of self-congratulation and of what matters about our work in times of confusion."[11] Schaar's "extolling of Puritan virtues"—"a bit odd" if endearing—manifests itself as a censorious moral conscience to which Euben looks for guidance, perhaps for reason that he fails to generate on his own the required pangs of remorse and humility that Schaar taught him marks the spirit of the thoughtful, serious theorist.[12] Further, Schaar's "richness of... mind is matched by the generosity of his friendship. Not the least pleasure of his friendship are the friends of his who have become mine, particularly Hanna Pitkin."[13] Pronouncements of friendship tend to shroud the true character of Euben's association with Schaar and Pitkin, namely, that he belongs to a cultish group of academics who share strong intellectual and emotional bonds and who make sharp distinctions between insiders and outsiders.

Euben tells us that Wolin is an "unexcelled teacher, able to help students do what they choose to do while leading them to recognize the implications of their choices";[14] and further, Wolin is a man whose "life and teachings... articulated the tensions present in political theory, demonstrating what it means to be intellectually serious and politically engaged...."[15] Euben thinks that Wolin is the pure opposite of a strong-willed, self-righteous and conformity-inducing master because he presumably cultivates independent thought among his students, "that our interests, style and conclusions are somewhat different is a testament to his teaching and friendship."[16] The key phrase here is "somewhat different." A difference can obviously be small, medium or large. Is the dissimilarity Euben points to a minor variation on themes of Wolin [or Schaar], or does he offer views that are independent of the strong imprint of Wolin's views?

We are assured that "if there is a 'Berkeley school' of political theory, it comes less from doctrine than from a sense of vocation he [Wolin] helped define and continues to exemplify."[17] Wolin presumably is quite unlike Strauss and Voegelin because he never set himself up as a patriarch of a school associated with strong, partisan teachings and political values that he preached to students in the process of cultivating disciples. Are we to think that Wolin's relative lack of doctrine but heightened "sense of vocation" makes him akin to Socrates, namely, a perplexed spirit who knows little or nothing but is still sufficiently wise to preach that the highest duty of people is to seek virtue and to care for their souls? Is Euben being ironical? I find it unimaginable that Wolin's "sense of vocation" is without a strong doctrinal core, if only because people with vocations usually have specific values and goals they want to actualize. Wolin can hardly be said to manifest religiosity without religion, style without content, or seeing without sight, as witnessed by his strong judgments, striking interpretations, and prophetic projections in *Politics and Vision*. And how could Wolin—who founded the now defunct *Democracy* as a forum for himself and his intellectually compatible associates and disciples to disseminate their ideas on how the American polity might be revivified—have mentally disconnected his "sense of vocation" from his political teachings and moral values?

The claim that Wolin taught "less doctrine" than a "sense of vocation" is contradicted by Euben himself in his preface to his *Tragedy of Political Theory* where he offers a brief but hostile treatment of Bloom's *Clos-*

ing of the American Mind—indeed, a treatment that is unoriginal and basically repeats the negative judgments that Wolin renders about Bloom in *Presence of the Past*.[18] After giving a short survey of Wolin's views on Bloom, I will show that Euben's criticisms clearly mirror his master's teaching, providing insight into the nature of the epigonic spirit in academic political theory.

Wolin thinks that Bloom gave the world a "dogmatic book guided by monumental prejudices" that expresses the "triumph of haute vulgarization..." and "marks the first exposure of 'Straussism' to a mass audience and vice versa."[19] Writing a "jazzy version of the works of Leo Strauss" signifies that Bloom has nothing new to say; he is merely an epigonic, dutiful disciple with a flair for striking language.[20] While Bloom's book is "reactionary in a literal sense"[21] because of its anti-populist values, it pretends otherwise by advocating a fantastic, bizarre vision of "democracy" understood as "equality of opportunity in a society ruled by a meritocratic elite."[22] Universities for Bloom should be isolated fortresses of aristocratic "high culture" protected from the destructive leveling pressures of the turbulent, ignorant masses.

For Wolin, student radicalism and feminist values of the 1960's, and the minority ethnic and racial politics of the 1990's, are special targets of Bloom's wrath because they embody a democratic spirit committed to "cultural relativism" that denies the reality of "absolute truth and objective standards," the essential foundation of philosophy, or "to what the epigones of Leo Strauss call philosophy."[23] Further, Bloom fails to see that the University is hardly an ivory tower of dispassionate aristocratic reflection, but instead is decisively shaped in its identity and values by "the needs of the economy, the pressures of corporations, or the policies of the state."[24] Bloom ultimately sides "with the social and political powers which have brought Universities to the condition he laments"[25] because he fails to grasp that education has become, according to Wolin, the preserve of anti-democratic capitalist and bureaucratic forces, with their values of specialization, efficiency, centralization, investment, profit, and mechanistic images of human organization.

Animated by Wolin's democratic, populist spirit, and by his theories of how the University is corrupted by bureaucratic, elitist values, Euben dances his master's tune and happily bashes Bloom, saying that his book "contributes to thoughtlessness; instead of enhancing the commitment to reason, it reinforces contempt for reason and fact; rather than exemplifying the theoretical life, it becomes part of a right-wing political agenda; instead of providing alternatives to what we have, it fits into a national mood made-up of equal parts nostalgia and revenge."[26] Further, Bloom is "less Socrates than an intellectual Rambo...,"[27] and is really an anti-democrat who sees "the sixties as an era of democratic excess in a society uncritically and thoroughly democratic...[whereas] we [read: Euben, Schaar and Wolin] saw 'pluralists' or 'democratic revisionists as anti-democrats who had co-opted democratic rhetoric and undermined democratic aspirations."[28] Euben voices Wolin's claim that Bloom rejects the values of the 1960's because he fears that populist social movements advocating democratic ideals would undermine the aristocratic calling of the University, and adds in Wolinian fashion that "the community of scholars was being debased not by students but by an administration that defined the University as a 'mechanism' held together by administrative rules and powered by money and faculty members who created an increasingly fragmented and specialized curriculum and who were more preoccupied with methodological purity, research strategies, and career trajectories than with teaching."[29] If there remains any doubt that Euben learned doctrine from his master, then consider the disciple's words about the 1960's in light of Wolin's analysis: "the University was already politicized, some of its faculty compromised by often unacknowledged ties to government and industry, its services offered to certain of the state's constituencies at the expense of others."[30]

Finally, Euben's inflated, epigonic portrayals of Wolin and Schaar as exemplary teachers and intellectuals strike me as partially private judgments shared by him and other committed disciples, and is his way of expressing gratitude, even repayment, for being aided by two famous and powerful masters in matters pertaining to career advancement.

Although Wolin is a passionate, erudite and powerful speaker in large undergraduate survey courses, it is unjust and inaccurate of Euben to call him an "unexcelled teacher," for this description hardly squares with his conduct of graduate seminars where he continuously lectured at small groups of students, rarely pausing to take questions or to facilitate class discussion. Further, Wolin became defensive when brighter students criticized his special interpretations of master-texts or of the "tradition" of political theory; and he was not above presenting rival scholarly ideas in a deliberately negative, unbalanced manner to clear the way for him to present his own authoritative views. Not a few students felt anxious when visiting Wolin during office hours: he seemed distant, unconcerned with their personal and intellectual problems, and often impatient to turn his attention to more weighty matters than conversing with them. If Wolin was for the most part neither particularly interested in, nor closely acquainted with a good many of his students' ideals and intellectual struggles, then Euben can hardly claim that Wolin helped "students do what they choose to do while leading them to recognize the implications of their choices."[31] Euben's epigonic mentality is prone to distort the truth.

Important qualities of Schaar as a teacher and scholar are missing in Euben's remarks. He leaves out how Schaar, unlike the tempermentaly cooler Wolin, sought adulation from, and closeness to, his students, and how that at Berkeley he placed himself on a moral plane above other faculty, projecting himself as a man of exemplary moral character, wit, and rare intelligence with a special vocation of "saving" the tradition of political theory from its enemies, whether these be empiricists or rival theorists. Some of Schaar's colleagues described him as "troublesome," "manipulative," a "pied piper," and "sophist" who used his personal charisma and image of being a unprofessional non-conformist to attract an "army" of students as "troops" in his and Wolin's battle to increase their Departmental power. Further, Schaar's love of friendship hardly extended to colleagues he contemptuously labeled as "academics" because, unlike himself, they presumably obeyed narrow, stifling professional norms and pursued trivial work. Perhaps more than Wolin, Schaar taught his students emnity toward the Straussians, of whom he said to me that they are "not like us."

Euben also says nothing about how Schaar was quick to voice strong "for's and against's" to his students, as if he possessed sublime truths and urgent moral convictions, while being quite willing to mold the young and unformed in his image. He spoke passionately of the need for "community," "friendship," "shared discourse" and "virtue," but these fine things were shared only by those he asked into his special circle of associates—his "friends"—an invitation signifying that the chosen were perceived as conforming to his strong moral and intellectual views, as well as being judged to be a person of "sound and good character." Schaar could be unkind and punishing toward real or imagined foes, but he always displayed charm, kindness and generosity toward his friends. Because both Schaar and Wolin saw themselves at Berkeley beset by evil-minded colleagues who conspired against them, they attempted to establish a separate Department of Political Theory where they and their "community" might lead a "shared intellectual life" devoted to the search for wisdom in an age they painted as a "wasteland." Schaar in particular wanted to defend "virtue" in the midst of what he described as "almighty corruption" and "fashion."

Of course covert and overt rivalry between academic schools of political theory are hardly limited to Wolin and his disciples criticizing "Straussism," although members of the so-called "Berkeley" school have a long history of antipathy to that teaching, manifest not only in vociferous critiques of it and some jealousy at its great institutional success, but also in the politics of appointment at UC Berkeley when two Straussians were denied tenure largely through the concerted efforts of Wolin and Schaar.

Still, permit me a few speculations. Both are characterized by the presence of enthusiastic, committed disciples who have strong feelings of community based on shared emotional and intellectual ties to them by a drive to remain as pure as possible in a world judged to be corrupt and in need of healing, and by members who see themselves as intrinsically different from, and superior to, persons who lack their wisdom.

Epigones of Strauss and Voegelin

For the epigonic, imitative spirit, the master is a heroic, wise person deserving the highest accolades and defense against indifference, misunderstanding and persecution. Academic political theory offers many examples. Thomas Pangle's preface to the *Rebirth of Classical Political Rationalism*[52] depicts Leo Strauss as an extraordinary doer of great deeds who alone in "the years between 1945 and 1970... seized a dull and dying academic discipline called the 'history of political ideas' and transformed it into an enterprise of gripping significance and vitality."[33] Feeling awe-struck in the presence of Strauss's feats, the disciple wishes to fathom the mystery of his master,

"What gave the history of political thought in his hands such a powerful allure? What is it about his writings that continues to shatter respectable intellectual categories and rules, thereby arousing so much fascination and so much hatred?"[34]

Pangle counsels readers of his master's works not to be deceived by "the initially historical or even pedantic appearance of Strauss's writing... [which] on closer inspection... is the sign of Strauss's powerfully incisive critical stance towards almost every major feature of the contemporary intellectual and political landscape."[35] The disciple assures the uncoverted that Strauss's dense, repetitive and circuitous style is mere surface; underneath is a rich and profound theoretical world that the disciplined and brave can learn to understand, at least with instruction by wise apostles.

Apparently most of us lack sufficient intellect and moral character to fathom Strauss's subtle meanings, and because we feel frustrated by our failure, we become hostile, judging him to be irritatingly obscure or nonsensical, "the prevalent scholarly reaction... has been censorious" of "Strauss's precedent shattering books," and "One is forced to wonder with a smile what moral and intellectual lapses this fellow has not been proven guilty of."[36] Pangle of course can ironically "smile" at unsympathetic or hostile outsiders because he is one of the *illuminati* who carries in his mind's eye Strauss's esoteric insights; as such, he gazes down from high at those dwelling below in the shadowy *doxa* world of the cave who fail to see that Strauss would free them from ignorance if only they would stop resisting and give their *psyches* over to proper instruction. And much as persons in the cave want to kill the philosopher who would break their chains of illusion, so Pangle thinks the "conventional guardians of culture and academe... rush to stamp out the fire that threatens their established peace and quiet."[37] Strauss, then, is a persecuted saviour of political theory.

A most revealing, and perhaps pathetic recitation of epigonic subservience, can be found in W.C. Havard writing in the preface to Eric Voegelin's *Search For Order*,[38] a collection of essays by Voegelin's disciples. Havard says that "I continue to experience the same pupil-teacher relationship with E. Voegelin that I have enjoyed for more than a quarter of a century"; and further, that remaining a dependent student is surely a "complement to him."[39] Does Havard remain a worshipful student because he finds it painfully difficult to make independent sense of the ambiguities and conflicts that are intrinsic to life and politics, and hence looks to Voegelin's "authoritative" knowledge for answers to his perplexities to calm his restless mind? Havard judges Voegelin "a man possessed of that rare quality of being able to look at things with a special vision not open to others until he had guided them toward it";[40] and the disciple feels overwhelmed by

172

his master's "awe-inspiring exploration of man's ubiq-
uitous search for the divine ground of being...."[41]
Havard's epigonic admiration for "Voegelin's continuing feats in mastering an ever-expanding volume and
variety of historical and philosophical materials..." [42]
signifies that because he has difficulty walking his own
path, and needs to identify with Voegelin to achieve
an intellectual and emotional center, he becomes the
master's worshipful epigone. We hear the usual refrain
that his teacher is not only ignored or misread, but
also dismissed with "categorical labels";[43] and because
he "is also far removed from the prevailing orthodoxy,
it is not surprising that many of his colleagues should
feel compelled to attack his position vociferously."[44]
Of course Havard and fellow disciples will keep the
master's faith and spend their lives defending him
against detractors rather than developing their own
capacity for autonomous, thoughtful judgement.

Germino's role as one of Voegelin's chief epigonic
champions is readily apparent in Beyond Ideology[45],
where he claims that his master is "a Columbus in the
realm of the spirit," at least for "many concerned with
the theoretical analysis of politics."[46] Who are these
"many"? Perhaps numbers of Voegelin's disciples
whose thought-processes are imprinted with the theoretical education they received from him or his leading disciples. And if Voegelin is the true "Columbus"
who discovered new continents for political theory,

or at least brought to light long forgotten ones, then it follows that other master-academics are of lower rank. For example, Bloom's claim in *Ancients and Moderns* that only "Leo Strauss has provided us with the scholarship and the philosophical insight necessary to a proper confrontation of ancients and moderns..."[47] implies that his master alone is the true Columbus. Cropsey in the same work says that "a great effort of scholarship and pedagogy has been necessary to bring this truth [the decline of political theory] to the attention of men in recent decades. Professor Strauss has been responsible for much of that effort."[48] We are led to wonder just how many Columbus's of intellect actually exist in our time?

Leaving aside the partisan issue of deciding which master-academic truly outshines the rest, Germino in the usual epigonic manner is upset that Voegelin's ground-breaking discoveries have been "ignored or systematically misunderstood," and partly for reason that he is not "read for what he has to teach."[49] Perhaps persons who worry about the "decline of political theory" have failed to welcome the "appearance of a thinker meticulously pointing the way to the recovery of political theory as a tradition of inquiry" [50] because, lacking the requisite intellectual and ethical sensitivities, they are unable to follow Voegelin to the New World to which he would lead us.

Germino's *Beyond Ideology* provides a fascinating

glimpse into the inability of the epigonic spirit to transcend blatant hero-worship and ideological prejudice in making judgments, and into the tendency of that spirit to see itself as having superior moral virtue and intellect compared to rival schools of political theory. The book's stated goal is to fathom how the ideas of Oakshott, Arendt, Jouvenal, Strauss, and Voegelin individually contribute to the recent "revival" of political theory; but unfortunately, with the exception of Voegelin, Germino's master, who is generously made the sole subject of a lengthy, fawning chapter, the others are given short-shrift by being lumped together and sketchily surveyed in a single chapter. The treatments of the five theorists—Wolin is ignored for some unexplained reason—are reminiscent of some hastily conceived Hegelian dialectic whereby the "Idea" of "revival" necessarily traverses from lower to higher stages of formulation, the highest of course being expressed by Voegelin who "later generations may well acclaim as the greatest political theorist of our time."[51]

Oakshott "scarcely qualifies as a complete political theorist"; he only prepares the way for Voegelin's "discovery of the transcendent," being himself unable "to cross over to that discovery."[52] And Arendt's "brilliance, erudition and insight" cannot save her from fatal "defects as a constructive political theorist," including having a "style" that is "on the obscure side" [whereas Voegelin's is lucid!], and from erroneously thinking that the "great political theory of the past can give us little assistance in constructing a 'new Humanism' or "clear guidelines for a new political theory."[53] Jouvenal fares somewhat better but is overly "reticent," his works being "essentially exploratory... for he does not do much more than intimate what the criteria are by which we measure the legitimate use of power," and he "fails to develop and clarify his support of a natural law position perhaps out of a belief... that the vocabulary of traditional political theory is no longer adequate to contemporary realities."[54] Strauss occupies a still higher position in Germino's grand scheme of viewing other master-academics as parts of a rational evolution toward Voegelin, for at least Strauss "raises the entire question of the relationship of theology to a new political science ...."[55] And if Strauss displays some "openness... to religious awareness," he ultimately fails because he, unlike Voegelin, "nowhere shows how theology and political philosophy can be related in a new political science properly understood."[56] Unfortunately, Germino's accounts of the defects and limitations of Oakshott, Jouvenal, Arendt, and Strauss presuppose a range of Voegelinian concepts, methods and standards of value that, in true epigonic fashion, guides his one-sided judgments.

It is controversial to draw analogies between religious sects and academic schools of political theory with respect to how charismatic authority functions in each. Not to be deterred, Shadia Drury writes: "to the unconverted, the Strauss of the Straussians had little appeal. If there was anything that made him the subject of curiosity, it was his uncanny ability to inspire apparently intelligent students with religious-like fervor and devotion."[57] Strauss, then, had some mysteriously magnetic power to generate power over students who should have known better than to be seduced into a unhealthy form of discipleship that blunted their critical faculties and transformed them into ideologues who defended his gospel. Drury clearly thinks that Straussians constitute a tight-knit group that distrusts outsiders who have not been initiated into their mysteries, and that the master's disciples made of him a demi-god worthy of unswerving veneration and loyalty.

One thing strikes me as certain: political theory in its institutionalized form is often indistinguishable from the quest for power, privilege and position, and perhaps Nietzsche was right to claim it is difficult for theorizing to avoid being a form of revenge or a will to tyrannize. Political theory, then, is ambiguous. It is the medium whereby some great spirits can potentially educate others to become discerning, critical, morally free, and genuinely caring about the fate of the body politic; but it can also become perverted, the preserve of a worshipful epigonic mentality that would lure us into intellectual blindness, moral insensitivity, and partisan fanaticism.

The study of masters and disciples can remind us of an easily forgotten truth, namely, that political theory, despite its self-understanding as an activity devoted to the life of the mind, shows itself entirely to be a "human, all too human" endeavor that cannot free itself from the failings, fears, dreams and sublime impulses of sometimes conscious beings who come into existence only to pass away again—beings who momentarily seek clarity in a universe that poses infinite questions and provides no ready answers.

Notes

Chapter One

1. *OED*, p. 689 (2.a.), vol. 17. *OED* references are to the *Oxford English Dictionary*, 2nd edition, Clarendon Press, Oxford, 1989. References abbreviated as *CEOED* are to the *Compact Edition of the Oxford English Dictionary*, Oxford University Press, 1971.
2. *EDEL*, p. 632. *EDEL* references are to the *Etymological Dictionary of the English Language*, Clarendon Press, Oxford, 1935.
3. *OED*, s.v. "teach" p. 688 (B.1.4.) vol. 17.
4. s.v. "teacher" p. 689 (I).
5. s.v. "teach" p. 688 (B.II.6.).
6. s.v. "mentor." p. 614, vol. 9.
7. (1.b.)
8. 1784 Cowper, Task II. 595.
9. 1814 Sir R. Wilson, *Priv. Diary* II. 329
10. 1869 Spurgeon, *Treas. David* (PS, xix. II) I.
11. 1879 *Expositor* IX. 462.
12. s.v. :tutor" (sb.), 1562 Pilkington, *Expos. Abdyas* 85.
13. 1616 Bullokar, *Eng. Expos., Tutour.*
14. c 1550 Becon *Catech.* VI Wks. 1564 I. 533 b.
15. Ibid.,
16. 1597 Hooker *Eccl.* Pol. V. lxxiii. 5.
17. Ibid.
18. Ibid.
19. 1701 Le Clerc's Prim Fthers (1702) 22.

20. Ibid.
21. 1653 *Register of Visitors Univ. Oxford* (1881) 360.
22. 1886. Willis and Clark *Cambridge* I. Introd. 91.
23. 1861 J.T. Coleridge *Publ. Sch. Educ.* 37.
24. Ibid., s.v. "tutor" (v.), 1740 J, Dupree *Conform. Anc and Mod. Cerem.* 39.
25. 1814 Chalmers *Evid. Chr. Revel.* x.292.
26. Ibid.
27. 1850 Maurice *Mor. and Met. Philos.* (1854) I. 9.
28. 1682 H. Penden in *Life* x. (1902) 209.
29. 1601 Weever *Mirr. Mart* fijb.
30. "tutorly" (a.), 1879 G. Mereidith *Egoist*,I. vi. 88.
31. *OR.* p. 384. *OR* references are to *Origins,* Macmillan Com pany, New York, 1961.
32. Ibid.
33. *OED*, s.v. "master" (sb.) p. 441 (I.1.a), vol. 9.
34. Ibid.
35. 1728 Swift *My Lady's Lament.* 174.
36. 1765 Blackstone *Comm.* I. xiv. 416.
37. 1554 in Strype Eccl. Mem. (1721) III. xxiiii. 190.
38. 1711 *Steele Spect.* no. 107, I.
39. Ibid.
40. Ibid.
41. 1863 Woolner *My Beautiful Lady* 64.
42. 1709 Steele *Tatler* no. 82 4
43. 1841 Lane *Arab.* Nts. I. 123
44. Ibid.
45. Ibid.
46. 1706 1691 Wood *Ath. Oxon.* I 101
47. 1706 Phillips (ed. Kersey), *Templars.*
48. Ibid.
49. Ibid.
50. 1850 Tennyson *In Mem.* lxxxvii I.
51. 1939 T.S. Eliot *Old Possum's Pract.* Cats 33.
52. Bunyan *Jerus. Sinner Saved* wks. (1845 73..
53. 1821 Suthey in *Q. Rev.* xxx. 310

54. Ibid.
55. Ibid.
56. 1711 *Addison Spect.* no, 129 I.
57. 1797 *Encycl. Brit.* (ed. 3) XIII. 615/2.
58. *ODEE*, p. 560. Reference are to the *Oxford Dictionary of English Etymology.*
59. *OED*, s.v. "master" p. 443 (II. 14) vol. 9.
60. Ibid, p. 442 II. (13.a.).   I
61. Ibid., (II. 11.).   I
62. 1711 Steele *Spect.* no 168 3.
63. 1771 Burke *Corr.* (1844)I. 284.
64. s.v. "hierophant."
65. Ibid.
66. 1774 Burney *Hist. Mus* (1789) I. 332
67. 1677 Hale *Prim. Orig. Man* II. xii 244
68. 1882 Whittier *Quest of Life* 5.
69. a 1882 Shelley *Def. Poetry* Pr. Wks 1888
70. 1843 J. Martineau *Chr. Life* (1867) 105.
71. s.v. "hierophantic" (a.), 1879 Mrs. Lynn Linton *Under Which Lord?* III. xi. 254
72. s.v. "master" (v.).p. 447
73. Ibid.
74. 1586 J. Hooker *Hist I Rel.* in Holinshed II 133/2
75. 1725 Watts *Logic* III. iii. 2.
76. 1841 James Brigand xx.
77. a 1623 Fletcher *Love's Cure* v. iii (1647)
78. s.v. "masterful" (a).p. 447.
79. s.v. :master" (v.).
80. Ibid.
81. 1740 J. Clarke *Educ. Youth* (ed. 3) 163.
82. 1865 Kingsley *Herew.*viii.
83. 1878 R.W. Dale *Lect. Preach.* iv 91.
84. *EDEL*, p. 610.
85. *CEDEL*, vol. 2, p. 1528. *CEDEL* refers to the *Comprehensive Etymological Dictionary of the English Language*, Elsevier Publishing Company, Amsterdam, 1967.

86. *ODEE*, p. 877. *ODEE* references are to the *Oxford Dictionary of English Etymology*, Clarendon Press, Oxford, 1966.
87. *OED*, s.v. "student" p. 976, vol. 16., 1660 I.H.B. *Valentine's Triumphant Chariot* 21
88. J. Hullah *Rudim. Mus. Gram.* 2
89. 1712 Steele *Spect.* no. 526   3
90. Ibid.
91. *EDEL*, p. 172.
92. *OED*, s.v. "disciple" (s6.) p. 733, vol. 4.
93. s.v. "master" (s6.)p. 442, vol. 9.
94. s.v. "disciple" (s6.) p. 733, vol. 4.
95. 1756 Nugent *Gr. Tour France* IV. 90.
96. 1893 *Chr. World* 16 Nov. 885/3.
97. 1711 Addison *Spect.* no. 163 para. 4.
98. *EV*, p. 308. *EV* references are to *Expanded Vine's*, Bethany House Publishers, Minneapolis, 1984.
99. *NTT*, p. 483, vol. 1. *NTT* references are *New Testament Theology*, three volumes, Paternoster Press, Exeter, 1975.
100. Ibid., p. 481.
101. Ibid.
102. Ibid., p. 490.
103. *OED*, s.v. "disciple" (v.) p. 734, vol 4.
104. a 1617 Hieron *Wks.* II. 482.
105. a 1711 Ken *Hymns Evang.* Poet. Wks. 1721 I. 179.
106. s.v. "discipline" (sb.).
107. s.v. "disciple" (v.).1596 Spencer F.Q. IV. Introd. I.
108. 1622 Drayton *Poly-olb.* xxiv. (1748) 356..
109. s.v. "discipline" (v.) p. 735.
110. Ibid.
111. Ibid.
112. s.v. "discipline" (v.).
113. s.v. "discipline" (sb.), 1892 Westcott *Gospel of Life* 270.
114. 1736 Butler Anal.1. v. wks 1874 I. 85.
115. *CEDEL*, p. 92, vol. 1.
116. *OED*, p. 556 s.v. "apostasy".
117. s.v. "apostate" (sb./a.). 1855 Milman *Lat. Chr.* (1864) IX.

XIV. I. 26..

118. s.v. "acolyte."

119 .1649 Selden *Laws of Eng*. I. X. (1739) 18.

120. 1873 W.H. Dixon *Two Queens* 1 vi x 369.

121. 1876 Chambers *Astron*. 910.

122. s.v. "*sycophant*" 1838 Thirwall Greece xxxi iv. 181.

123. 1561 B. Googe Palingenius' *Zodaic of Life to Rdr*.

124. s.v. "sycophancy" 1850 Grote *Greece* II lxv. (1862) v. 562.

125. "sycophant."

126. a1633 Austin *Medit*. (1635) 224.

127. Prescott *Mexico* II.i (1850) I. 183.

128. 1736 Bolingbroke *Patriot*, 139.

129. 1877 Mrs. Oliphant *Makers Flor*. x. 252

130. s.v. "sycophantic" (a.), 1854 J.S.C. Abbot *Napoleon* (1855) II. I. 24.

131. "sycophant" (s.b.), 1692 E. Walker tr. *Epictetus' Mor., In PraiseEpictetus*.

132. a 1700 Evelyn *Diary* 25 Mar. 1657.

133 .s.v. "sycophancy" 1657 Trapp *Comm. Esther* iii. I.

134. 1860 Mill Repr. Govt. (1865) 67/I.

135. ODEE, s.v. "cult," p. 234.

136. Ibid., p. 234; s.v. "colony," p. 192.

137. Ibid., s.v. "wheel," p. 1001.

138. *OED*, s.v. "cultus" 1865 Pusey *Truth Eng*. ch. 181.

139. s.v. "cult" (sb.), 1859 L. Oliphant *China and Japan* I. xii. 242.

140. Ibid.

141. 1679 Penn *Addr. Prot*. II. App. 245.

142 .1711 Shaftesb. 142 *Charac*. III. I (1737) I. 281.

143. s.v. "cultivate" (v.).

144. 1681-6 J. Scott *Chr.Life* (1747) III. 377.

145 .1713 Addison *Cato* I.

146. Ibid.

147. Ibid.

148. Ibid. 7

149.1707 Collier *Refl. Ridic*. 215.

15.0 s.v. "culture" (sb.) 1483 Caxton *Gold Leg.* 81/1.

151. 1665-9 Boyle *Occas. Refl.* (1675) 320.

152. 1856 Emerson *Eng. Traits, Ability* wks (Bohn) II. 42.

153. Ibid.

154. c1510 More *Picus Wks.* 14.

155. 1651 Hobbes *Leviath.* II. xxxi. 189.

156. 1867 Freeman *Norm, Conq.* (1876) I. iv. 150.

157. s.v. "culture" (v.), 157 1776 S.J. Pratt *Pupil Pleas.* II. 89.

158. s.v. "sect."

159. Ibid.

160. Ibid.

161. Ibid.

162. Ibid.

163. Ibid.

164. 1667 Milton P.L. VI. 147.

165. 1542-3 *Act 34 and 35 Hen.* VIII, c.i.

166. 1560 Daus tr. *Sleidane's Comm.* 81.

167. 1776 Adam Smith W.N. v. I. (1869) II. 377.

168. 1676 Glanvill *Ess.* V. 24.

169. s.v. "sectarian" (s6) 1685 Bunyan *Pharisee and Publ.* 7.

170. 1860 Motley *Netherl.* ii (1868) I. 25.

171. s.v. "sect," a 1591 H. Smith *Arrow agst. Atheists* (1637) 18.

172. 1693 Dryden *Persius* I. Argt.

173. 1868 Farrar *Seekers After God, Seneca* Intro. 5.

174. 1776 Adam Smith W.N. v. ii (1869) II. 420.

175. a 1711 Ken *Hymnotheo*, Poet, Wks. 1721 III. 389.

176. 1861 J. Edkins in Mrs. Edkins *Chinese Scenes* (1863) 273.

177. 1530 Tindale *Prol. I Cor.*

178. s.v. "sectarian" 1836 Lytton *Athens* (1837) II. 416.

179. 1650 Rec. *Comm. Gen. Assembly* (S.H.S.) III. 92.

180. 1828 P. Cunningham *N.S. Wales* (ed. 3) II 244.

181. Ibid.

182. Ibid., s.v. "sectary" (ab./a.), 1824 Landor *Imag. Cnv., Jas. I and Casubon Wks.* 1846 I. 30.

183. s.v. "sectarian," 1827 Carlyle *Germ. Rom.* IV. 22.

184. "sectary." 1771 *Lett. Junius* lix (1788) 314.

185. 1869 A. Harwood tr. *E. de Pressense's Early Yrs*. Chri. III. ii. 378.
186. 1860 Motley *Netherl.* ii (1868) I 27.
187. 1762-71 H. Walpole *Vertue's Anecd. Paint.* (1786) III. 2.
188. 1605 Marston *Dutch Courtezan* III.
189. 1808 Syd. Smith *Methodism* wks. 1859 I 88/I.
190. Ibid.
191. 1589 R. Harvey *Pl. Perc.* 7.
192. 1609 Holland *Amm. Marcell.* 109.
193. 1704 N.N. tr. *Boccalini's Advts Fr. Parnass.* III. 146.
194. 1638 Ld. Digby *Lett. conc. Relig.* (16751) 3.
195. 1798 Edgeworth *Pract. Educ.* (1811) II. 427.
196. s.v., "sectator," 1541 R. Copland *Galylen's Terap.* 2d ijb.
197. 1585 t. Washington tr. *Nicholay's Voy.* III. xxii. 112.
198. 1614 Raleigh *Hist. World* I. iii. I. 33.
199. 1664 Evelyn tr. *Freart's Archit.* I. vi. 22.
200. 1888 Doughty *Arabia Deserta* I. 264.
201. s.v. :votary" (sb.).
202. 1662 Owen *Animadv. Fiat Lux* v. wks. 1855 xiv. 68.
203. a1596 *Sir T. More* III. ii.
204. 1682 Villiers (Dr. Buckhm..) *Chances V*. iii.
205. a 1700 Ken *Sion* Poet. Wks. 1721 iv. 388.
206. a 1690 Prior *To Earl of Dorset* i.
207. 1738 Gray *Propertius* I. 2.
208. 1869 Freeman *Norm. Conquest* (1875) III. xiv. 360.
209. 1764 Reid Inquiry I. 8.
210. 1771 Beattie *Minstr.* I. ix.
211. 1806 H.K. White *Lett.* (1837) 319.
212. 1873 Hamerton *Intell.* Life VI. iv. 218.
213. 1811 Shelley *St. Irvyne* iii.
214. 1783 Cowper *Valediction* 71.

Chapter Two

1. *Nicomachean Ethics*, bk. VI. ch. 4, trans. J.A. Thompson, (Baltimore, Penguin, 1966). For further comments of the nature of craft knowledge: bk. I, ch. 7, bk. II, ch. 6; bk. VI, chs. 4, 5, 6.

2. *NE*, bk. III, ch. 3. For further comments on the nature of practical wisdom: bk. I, chs. 2, 3, 5; bk. II, ch. 6; bk. III, ch. 3; bk. VI, chs. 2, 5, 7-10, 13; bk. X, chs. 7, 8, 9.

3. *NE*, bk. 10. ch. 7. For further comments on the nature of contemplative wisdom: bk I, ch. 6; bk 6, chs. 1, 3, 6, 7, 12; bk. 10, chs. 7, 8. Aristotle's sharp separation of theoretical and practical wisdom, of contemplation from politics, leads to the impossibility of deducing, from the eternal Ideas, universal moral precepts and unchanging institutional forms. In short, the cosmic and variable realms of being have no point of mediation to be politically relevant. See the *Nichomachean Ethics*, bk. I, ch. 6 for Aristotle's criticism of Plato's concept of the Forms as "embracing both the absolutely and the relatively good"; and bk. VI. ch. 7 for his claim that "wisdom cannot be identified with political science." Also: *Politics*, bk. I. chap. 1 for his claim that Plato confused the statesman with "the monarch of a kingdom, or the manager of a household"; bk. II, chs. 2-4 for his discussion of how his teacher's views on the unity of the *polis* violates the natural diversity of political association; and bk. III, ch. 4 for Aristotle's contention that a great gulf must exist between the unchanging qualities of the "good man" and those contingent ones that mark the "good citizen."

4. Of course not every master of philosophy claims to possess wisdom or to want disciples, as witnessed by Plato's depiction of Socrates in the *Apology* as a perplexed man who "knows nothing" about supremely important moral, political and cosmic matters; and who, in the presence of his companions, passionately searches for truth about how to best live. Further, a master may

also reject having adherents for fear they will corrupt his teaching or fail to walk their own paths in life, much as Nietzsche's Zarathustra warns potential disciples to leave his presence and seek their own spiritual and intellectual centers—to become masters in their own right—before they may fruitfully discourse together in the spirit of equality and friendship. However, it is possible that Socrates and Nietzsche might have, as consummate ironicists and wearers of masks, rejected discipleship as a ploy to distinguish themselves from rival teachers of wisdom who actively sought followers, and even to make themselves mysteriously seductive to persons they really wished to teach.

Chapter Four

1. *NTT*, p. 759.
   New York, 1969.
2. Ibid.
3. Ibid, p. 760.
4. *SV*, p. 213. SV references are to *Sacramentum Verbi*, Herder and Herder, New York, 1969.
   5. 95. *Lk.* 4:16-12; *Mk.* 12:13-34; *Mk.* 3:13-19; *Jn.* 6:66-69; *Acts* 16:22; *Mt.* 9:35; *Mk.* 12:35; *Lk.* 21:37; *Mt.* 26:55; *Jn* 18:20; and *Mt.* 5:2, *Mk* 6:34; *Lk* 5:3.
6. *Mt.* 4:18-22, 10:6; *Mk.* 2:14; *Lk.* 10:6.
7. *Mt.* 10; *Mk.* 6:6-11; *Lk.* 9:15, 10:1-13.
8. *Lk.* 9:59-14:26; *Jn.* 6:66; *Mk.* 3:31-5.
9. *Mt.* 10-:37; *Jn.* 11:16; *Mk.* 1:16-20.
10. *Mk.* 3:14; *Lk.* 13:22-30; *Mt.* 3:14, 10:37, 23:8; *Lk.* 13:22-30, 14:27.102. *DJG*, p. 809. *DJG* refers to *Dictionary of Jesus and the Gospels*, Intervarsity Press, Leicester, 1956.
11. *Mk.* 10:32; *Mt.* 10:24f, 16:24; *Lk.* 18:34.
12. *Mk.* 10:32; *Mt.* 10:24f, 16:24; *Lk.* 18:34.
13. *Mk.* 4:10, 10:13, 14:47; *Mt.* 13:36, 16:22; *Lk.* 18:34..
14. *OED*, vol. IX, p. 442

15. Ibid.
16. *DJG*, p. 810.
17. Ibid, vol. 4, p. 733.
18. Ibid.
19. Ibid.
20. Mircea Eliade, ed., *Encyclopedia of Religion*, (Macmillan, New York, 1987), vol. 14, p. 19. Hereafter cited as ER.
21. Ibid, p. 30.
22. John Gordon, ed., *Encyclopedic Dictionary of Yoga*, (Paragon House, New York, 1990), p. 123.
23. *ER*, vol. 14, p. 33.
24. *Adavaya-Taraka Upanishad* (14).
25. *Guru Tattva*, (Divine Life Society, Himalayas, India, 1976), p. 26. Hereafter cited as GT.
26. Ibid.
27. Ibid, p. 4.
28. Ibid, p. 3.
29. Ibid.
30. *Yoga-Kundaly Upanishad*, III. 17.
31. *EDY*, p. 125.
32. *Guru Nanak*, (Indraprastha Press, New Dehli, 1982), p. 47.
33. *GT*, p. 4.
34. Ibid, p. 5.
35. Ibid, p. 6
36. Ibid.
37. Ibid.
38. Ibid.
39. Ibid, p. 25.
40. Ibid, p. 12.
41. Ibid, p. 15.
42. Ibid, p. 16.
43. Ibid.
44. Ibid, p. 19.
45. Ibid.
46. Ibid, p. 22.
47. Ibid, p. 94.

48. Ibid, p. 63.
49. Ibid, p. 72.
50. Ibid, p. 21.
51. *Saura-Purana,* LXV 111.11.
52. *Mahabharata,* X11 159. 46.
53. *GT,* p. 4.
54. Ibid, p. 93.
55. *Shiva-Samhita,* III.11; 13.
56. *GT,* p. 47.
57. *Kula Arnava Tantra,* X111. 106.
58. *Shiva-Samhita,* III. 11; 13.
59. *GT,* p. 7.
60. Ibid, p. 8.
61. Ibid, p. 47.

Chapter Five

1. Compact Edition Oxford English Dictionary, I., p.241
2 . Ibid.
3. Eduard Bernstein, Evolutionary Socialism, (New York: Schocken, 1961), p. 200. Notes one through sixteen are to ES
4. p. 25.
5. Ibid.
6. p. 26.
7. p.103.
8 . Preface, xxv
9. p. 39.
10. pp. 85-6.
11. p. 34.
12. Ibid.
13. p. 219.
14. pp. 204-5.
15. Preface to English edition, xxi.

16. Preface, xxxi.

17. Preface, xxx.

18. Ibid.

19. Ibid.

20. Ibid.

21. Quoted in Daniel Halevy, The Life of Friedrich Nietzsche, (New York: Macmillan, 1911), p. 58.

22. Letter to Carl von Gersdorff, August 4, 1869

23. Letter to Richard Wagner, May 21, 1870

24. Letter to Richard Wagner, May 22, 1869

25. Wagner in Bayreuth, trans. R.J. Hollingdale in Untimely Meditations, (Cambridge: Cambridge University Press, 1983), pp. 208-9.

26. Ecce Homo, in Collected Works, pp. 743-4.

27. Letter to Elizabeth Nietzsche, August 18.

28. Human, All Too Human, trans. Marion Faber, (Lincoln: University of Nebraska Press, 1984), Preface, p. 4. Notes eight through twenty-three are to Nietzsche's Preface.

29. pp.4-5.

30. p. 10.

31. p. 6.

32. Ibid.

33. Ibid.

34. Ibid.

35. Ibid.

36. Ibid.

37. Ibid.

38. p. 7.

39. Ibid.

40. Ibid.

41. Ibid.

42. Ibid.

43. p. 8. Nietzsche worried that his demand for a complete "re-adjustment of our most venerated sentiments" could be wrongly perceived as a call to moral license and an appeal to "unsuitable types" (Nietzsche to Malwida Von Meysenbug, April 16, 1884).

To protect his teaching, Nietzsche developed subtle ways of filtering out undesirable readers—potential disciples—who lacked spiritual readiness to hear his "terrible truths", or worse, who might pervert his "wild wisdom." His aphoristic and self-contradictory style, his abundant irony, his shrill tones and sensational claims, were all intended to frustrate most readers, to force them to back away in despair or nervous laughter, "our highest insights must—and should—sound like follies and sometimes like crimes by those who are not predisposed and predestined for them" (Beyond Good and Evil, trans. Walter Kaufman in Collected Works, p. 232).

A challenge was issued by Nietzsche to his readers to fathom his true self beyond his projected masks, "Every profound spirit needs a mask... around every profound spirit a mask is continuously growing, owing to the constantly false, namely, shallow, interpretation of every word, of every step, of every sign of life he gives"(BGE, p. 240). A reader with weakness of intellect, poverty of feeling and self-deceptive instincts is excluded "once and for all" from hearing "the first language for a new series of experiences" (Ecce Homo, trans. W. Kaufman in Collected Works, p. 717).

Nietzsche's attitude creates some dilemmas. How might he educate people to the dangers of nihilism if he made it very difficult for them to understand his theories, and further, how might he attract worthy followers who might begin the process of the "transvaluation" of values? He gave no clear answers, but still hoped a time would come when "a few men" appear "who can fully appreciate what I've done" (Nietzsche to Malwida Von Meysenbug, April 16, 1884). The "few" who might fathom his philosophy must first prepare their spirits, and test their worth, by surviving a series of difficult experiences.

> To those human beings who are of any concern to me I wish suffering, desolation, sickness, ill-treatment, indignities—I wish that they should not remain unfamiliar with profound self-contempt, the torture of self-mistrust, the wretchedness of the van-

quished: I have no pity for them, because I wish them
the only thing that can prove today whether one is
worth anything or not—[that one stands firm]"(*Will
to Power*, trans. W. Kaufman, p.481).

The phrase, dab er standhalt—the final words of the passage
are translated by Kaufman as "that one endures." I have substi-
tuted "that one stands firm" as more in Nietzsche's spirit. The
verb, standhalten, signifies constancy, holding out, resisting and
withstanding. I cannot imagine that Nietzsche merely wanted
thoughtful persons to passively endure their age, but rather, to
stand firm against it as an affirmation of nobility and self-will.
Mere endurance is for the passive, suffering beast of burden, the
camel, whereas the lion actively asserts his power even while suffering. See the parable of the "Three Metamorphoses" in Thus
Spake Zarathustra, I. Of course not all masters erect such obstacles to having disciples, and I imagine that Nietzsche's attitude toward potential followers was powerfully shaped by his recognizing the self-destructive character of his seduction by Wagner's
vision of cultural renewal and by his uncritical infatuation with
Schopenhauer's philosophy.

Chapter Six

1. It was during Schaar and Wolin's years of personal and intellectual collaboration that the "Berkeley School" evolved the distinctive identity the two impressed on their students, who, in some
instances, gained faculty positions and instructed new generations of learners in the ideas and ideals of their masters. [Schaar
and Wolin's jointly authored articles are collected in *The Berkeley
Rebellion and Beyond: Essays in Politic and Education in the Techno-
logical Society,* The New York Review, 1970]. Also, Hanna Pitkin's
intellectual and personal contributions to the school, although
coming somewhat after Schaar and Wolin began collaborating,
are hardly negligible, given that she is Wolin's prize student and

former colleague, and initially Schaar's friend and later his wife. The "Berkeley School" appears more loosely organized than those founded by Strauss and Voegelin, partly the consequence of its decentralized, populist ethos and lack of a single dominant charismatic leader. The school, then, has a few "heads of household" whose personal relationships and degrees of influence may vary dynamically over time, although Pitkin, Schaar and Wolin remain bound by common traditions, modes of discourse and conceptions of theorizing that stamp them as a distinctive academic "sodality"—to use Wolin's word.

2. Strauss, *Presence of the Past,* p. 51.

3. Ibid.

4. Ibid.

5. Ibid.

6. Ibid.

7. Ibid.

8. Euben's tendency to use Wolin's teachings as paradigmatic for his own work is also found in *Greek Tragedy and Political Theory,* (Berkeley: U.C. press, 1986) where he says in part 4 of his introductory chapter: "my text is Sheldon Wolin's 'Political Theory as a Vocation.' Because the essay suggests and displays affinities between theory and tragedy, it serves as a preface to my outline of what a dialogue between Greek tragedy and contemporary political theory might accomplish" (p. 7). Euben's reliance on Wolin's tenets to formulate the relevance of tragedy to the task of theorizing in our age is found on pp. 32 ff.

9. Princeton, 1990.

10. Transaction Books, 1981.

11. Preface, xiii.

12. Ibid.

13. Ibid.

14. Preface, xiii.

15. Ibid.

16. Ibid.

17. Preface, xiii-xiv.

18. John Hopkins, 1989.

19. p. 50.
20. p. 51.
21. p. 52.
22. p. 53.
23. p. 54.
24. p. 55.
25. p. 54.
26. Preface, xi.
27. Ibid.
28. p. xiv.
29. Ibid.
30. Ibid.
31. Ibid.
32. University of Chicago, 1989.
33. Introduction, vii.
34. Ibid.
35. Introduction, viii.
36. Introduction, ix.
37. Ibid.
38. Ed., E. McKnight, Louisiana State University Press, 1978.
39. p. 1.
40. p. 10.
41. p. 25.
42. p. 2.
43. p. 2.
44. p. 12.
45. Harper, 1967.
46. p. 162.
47. p. 240.
48. Preface, viii.
49. p. 161.
50. Ibid.
51. p. 131.
52. p. 142.
53. p. 144.
54. p. 156.

55. p. 160.
56. Ibid.
57. "Reply to My Critics," *Vital Nexus*, 1:1, May, 1990, p. 133.